Wendy Knits Lace

Wendy Knits Lace

Essential Techniques and Patterns for Irresistible Everyday Lace

Wendy D. Johnson

POTTER
CRAFT

NEW YORK

Library of Congress Cataloging-in-Publication Data

Johnson, Wendy D.
   Wendy knits lace : essential techniques and patterns
for irresistible everyday lace / Wendy D. Johnson. --
1st ed.
      p. cm.
   Includes index.
   ISBN-13: 978-0-307-58667-4 (alk. paper)
   ISBN-10: 0-307-58667-7 (alk. paper)
1. Knitted lace--Patterns. I. Title.
   TT800.J65 2011
   746.2'26--dc22
                                        2011000320

ISBN 978-0-307-58667-4

Printed in China

Cover and interior design by La Tricia Watford
Photographs by Alexandra Grablewski
Illustrations by Kara Gott Warner and
veést Design

The author and publisher would like to thank the
Craft Yarn Council of America for providing the
yarn weight standards and accompanying icons
used in this book. For more information, please
visit www.YarnStandards.com.

10 9 8 7 6 5 4 3 2 1

First Edition

Contents

Introduction

I love to knit lace. I love that a single skein of yarn, which can be an inexpensive investment, gives me many, many hours of knitting entertainment. What's more, lace projects have a high "wow" factor: The simplest of stitches, when combined in lacework, produce complicated-looking finished patterns that always seem to amaze. Perhaps that's why I found myself creating lots of fun lace sock patterns to fit all kinds of feet in my last two books, *Socks from the Toe Up* and *Toe-Up Socks for Every Body*.

My first attempt at lace knitting, I have to admit, was not a success. When I was an enthusiastic but inexperienced teenaged knitter, I eagerly grabbed yarn and needles and jumped right into a pattern for a lacy tank top. Never mind that I had absolutely no experience knitting lace. I barely knew what a yarn over was and, not surprisingly, ran into problems on the first row of the lace pattern; I could not complete it without creating extra stitches. Stubborn knitter that I was (and still am), I refused to ask for help. I spent an entire day knitting and ripping out the same row until I abandoned the project in frustration.

Fifteen years passed before I dared tackle a major lace project again—this time, a wedding handkerchief knit in cobweb-weight wool on size 0000 (1.25mm) needles. With years of knitting experience and some specific instruction in lace techniques on my side, I completed the handkerchief project successfully—although I did puncture my fingertips with the tiny needles a few times and sprain my wrist in a rather overzealous blocking of the piece. As you might guess, by then I was head over heels in love with lace and went on to knit many incredibly fine shawls of cobwebby lace that are as light as a cloud. Although they are beautiful, these fragile creations are not exactly practical for everyday use and, unfortunately, usually are kept carefully folded in a drawer.

The pieces I use over and over again are sturdier lace. The shawls and scarves I knit from slightly heavier lace-weight yarns and sock yarns, for example, are the ones I wear all winter long. I like the idea of knitting pieces that are sturdy and serviceable while at the same time lacy and pretty—lace for everyday life.

In this book, you will find lace you'll want to live in, too. Most of the patterns do not use yarns that are considered truly lace-weight—those incredibly fine, gossamer strands that look as though they would break if you looked at them the wrong way or tangle and knot if you looked away for a second—but heavier lace-weight, fingering-weight, DK-weight, and worsted-weight yarns so that you can knit (and wear) lace through all four seasons.

If you are new to lace, you'll find everything you need to master this type of knitting. In Part 1, you will learn how to choose the most appropriate needles and yarn, read a lace chart, quickly catch and fix errors, and finish and block a project. Even the most intricate-looking lace pattern can be surprisingly easy to knit, once you learn a few basics. In Part 2 (page 21), you will learn all the techniques needed to knit the projects in this book, with all the stitches used and then some. Then in Part 3 (page 39), twenty projects will test your new lace-knitting skills, including a delicate camisole for layering, a pullover sweater for staving off a chill on an autumn afternoon, mittens for winter, and—yes—some shawls and stoles to knit in whatever weight yarn you choose. Of course, I've also got your feet covered with my latest designs for pretty and practical toe-up socks! The patterns have something for everyone, at every skill level. Finally, yarn weights, abbreviations, and more are presented in the Resources section (page 137).

So whether you are knitting lace for the first time or just looking for new patterns to sink your needles into, I hope that this book inspires you to knit beautiful lace creations that you'll wear every day.

— PART 1 —

UNDERSTANDING THE BASICS

Lace is created from what is not there: negative space, created by a series of holes that form patterns and motifs. Although lace may look complex and mysterious, anyone who can read a chart and work decreases and yarn overs can create beautiful lace.

Knitting lace does not require a lot of special equipment, but choosing the most appropriate needles and yarn, for example, will make your lace knitting more enjoyable and successful. This section contains guidance about the tools needed for knitting lace, a tutorial on working from charts, instructions for blocking your finished lace piece, and a toolkit of tips and tricks for preventing and fixing mistakes.

NEEDLES

You might be thinking, *Do I really need special needles to knit lace?* Although, technically, you could knit lace on any old needles you have lying around, I guarantee that you will find knitting lace to be a far more enjoyable experience when you use the most appropriate needles for the project. For some projects, you can choose needle type (straight or circular), but for all projects, your choice should take into account three basic needle characteristics: material; "pointy-ness" of the tips; and, if using circulars, the smoothness of the join.

When you must choose between straight and circular needles, consider your project carefully. How many stitches will you be knitting in a row at the widest point? What are the thickness and the weight of the yarn that you will be using? These characteristics will determine not only how wide your work will be—and how many stitches will have to fit on the needles—but also how heavy the work will become after you really get going.

Long straight needles, hundreds of stitches, or heavier-than-lace-weight yarn can place undue strain on hands or wrists, making knitting more of a painful chore than a relaxing pastime. Whereas a scarf or other similarly narrow piece might be knit comfortably on straight needles, a large piece like a shawl generally would be easier to knit on a circular needle.

After you have chosen your needle type, think about how you want your needles to perform. Knitting needles are made from metal, wood, or plastic. If you are going for speed, choose metal—it's slick, and stitches move smoothly and quickly along a slick surface. However, slick metal needles also can allow your stitches to slide right off the tips if you're not careful! If you are new to lace knitting, choose wood or plastic needles because they have a little bit of "grab." Your stitches will not slide quite as smoothly as on metal but will be much more likely to stay where they belong.

KNITTING FULL CIRCLE

Let me tell you right up front, I knit almost exclusively with circular needles.

I find them easier and more convenient to use than straight needles—to me, there is nothing amusing about jamming 300-plus stitches onto 14-inch (35.5cm) straight needles. My stitches spread out nicely along the cable of a circular needle, which results in a more even weight distribution between my hands and thus a more comfortable knitting experience.

What's more, I can see my design better because all the stitches aren't squished together. Icing on the cake? I don't have to buy multiple types of needles in the same sizes.

But just because I stubbornly insist that circular needles are best—and there is no way you can convince me otherwise!—doesn't mean that you have to use them, too.

Even more important than needle material, however, is the pointy-ness of the needles' tips. Lace knitting involves making countless decreases (to account for the countless increases that create that oh-so-lovely negative space), often working two or three stitches together. The pointier the needle, the easier it will be to work your decreases.

Finally, if you have decided to use a circular needle, choose one that has smooth joins between the flexible cable and the solid needles. Few things are more frustrating in knitting than snagging a delicate lace yarn on a rough or loose join. I have painful memories of knitting a shawl a number of years ago that required "knit 3 together" maneuvers on every single row of the pattern, so I chose to use the pointiest circular needle I owned in the correct size at the time. Unfortunately, this circular also had loose joins, and I spent the entire lace project picking the fine lace-weight yarn out of the gap between needle and cable—and fearing for my sanity. Thankfully, many brands of circular needles are available that have sharp points and nice smooth joins.

YARNS

Lace can be knit from yarns of any weight; a yarn does not have to be designated "lace-weight" to be appropriate. Lace also can be knit from yarns of many natural fibers, including wool, silk, cashmere, alpaca, mohair, bamboo, or even some of the newer yarns made, for example, from seaweed or milk protein. The natural elasticity of these fibers allows for easy blocking (page 13), which stretches the stitches and opens up the lacework in the design.

I've intentionally left two kinds of yarn off the list for lace knitting: acrylic and cotton. Yarns with an acrylic content of more than 20 percent will not block well; instead, they will return to the original shape of the piece, closing up all the open stitchwork that you worked so hard to create and that makes lace so, well, lacy. Yarns with a high cotton content present problems both on the needles and off. Cotton has no elasticity or "give" and can be difficult to work with when knitting a pattern with a lot of decreases—like lace—and, once completed, a cotton piece has a tendency to stretch and sag from its own weight. That said, don't give up on acrylic and cotton fibers completely. Many wool-blend yarns that include a small percentage of acrylic fiber work just fine for lace knitting (for example, many sock yarns are 80 percent wool and 20 percent nylon); the natural fiber content is high enough to compensate for the undesirable properties of the acrylic. The same is true for a cotton-blend yarn that contains at least 25 percent wool or stretchy microfiber.

My rule of thumb for yarn choice? There is no rule of thumb. So if you have a lovely, unidentified yarn or a yarn of questionable makeup that you wish to turn into a lacy work of art, knit a lace-patterned swatch and block it. Spending a little extra time up front might save you a lot of work and heartache!

CHARTS

Most lace patterns are knit from charts, including the patterns in this book. On a pattern chart, each stitch is represented by a symbol, which might translate to anything from "k" to "sl1, k2tog, psso"—so you can see how the shorthand might be helpful. However, I know that charts can be a deal breaker for some knitters—if a pattern is worked from charts, they won't knit it—so if you are chart-phobic, I encourage you to read this section. After you have learned how to read a pattern chart you'll understand that, for knitting lace, charts are so much easier than written-out patterns.

Most of my patterns use simple stitch combinations and are easy to memorize; just use the symbol keys included with each project or refer to the master Key to Symbols (page 139) in the Resources section.

how to knit from a chart

The direction of reading a knitting chart is the exact opposite of reading text; you begin reading at the bottom right corner and work your way to the top left. When knitting a flat piece, you work the first (bottom) row of the chart (right side) from right to left, turn your work, then work the second row of the chart (wrong side) from left to right. **Note: When knitting in the round, every chart row is a right-side row worked from the right to the left.**

The sample chart and key on this page is for a lace pattern that is 6 stitches across and 6 rows long.

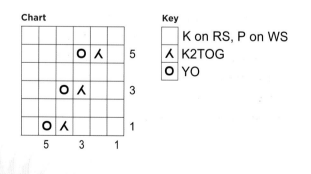

Chart

Key

	K on RS, P on WS
人	K2TOG
O	YO

Look at row 1, which is a right-side row. In words, row 1 is worked as follows: Knit 3, knit 2 together, yarn over, knit 1 (6 stitches worked). Next, let's see how these words are translated to symbols on the chart. The first 3 squares are blank, and on the key, you will see that a blank square designates a knit stitch on the right side of your work (and a purl stitch on the wrong side), so knit 3. The symbol in the next square means "knit 2 together," so that's what you do. Then the symbol for the fifth stitch means "yarn over," so work a yarn over. Then knit 1 stitch as designated by the last blank square. **Note: Although you decreased 1 stitch (by knitting 2 stitches together), the 1-stitch increase (yarn over) compensates for that loss so the total number of stitches on the needle should be the same at the end of the row as at the beginning.**

The written pattern will tell you how many times to work the chart, sometimes referred to as how many "pattern repeats" to work. For example, if your piece is 24 stitches wide and your pattern extends all the way across the piece, you would work each 6-stitch repeat 4 times across each row.

On the chart, row 2 is shown as a plain "knit across" row. If you are working a flat piece and have turned your work, you will *purl* all the way across, because the key tells you that the blank square represents a purl stitch on the wrong side of the work. (This is the general rule for charts for flat knitting.) If you are knitting in the round, however, you would *knit* across row (or round) 2, because the right side always faces you when knitting in the round.

Continue working the pattern according to the chart, repeating each row 4 times over your 24 stitches, and purling each wrong-side row:
Row 3: Knit 2, knit 2 together, yarn over, knit 2.
Row 4: Purl across.
Row 5: Knit 1, knit 2 together, yarn over, knit 3.
Row 6: Purl across.

After you have completed these 6 rows, your pattern may direct you to work the chart again, which would mean starting with row 1 and working another 6 rows total. You will continue in this manner until you have reached the length required by the pattern.

With a little practice, you will soon find that knitting from charts is easy. The charts for the patterns in this book are all straightforward, and any additional information you need to knit from a particular chart is included in the pattern instructions. For example, for projects knit from several charts, the pattern specifies exactly which chart you will use for each section. For some of the shawl projects, you will knit across several charts per row, and the order is spelled out clearly in the pattern instructions.

SWATCHES AND GAUGE

When you choose a new project you are, of course, eager to cast on. Why bother to knit a gauge swatch, particularly if you are knitting an unfitted piece of lace, like a shawl? First and foremost, a swatch gives you a good idea of how your yarn will work with your pattern. You might discover, for example, that the fuzzy mohair yarn that looked so pretty in the skein obscures your lace pattern, or that triple decreases are too much trouble in a slippery silk yarn. By knitting a swatch, you will save yourself the disappointment and frustration of ending up with a project that does not turn out as you envisioned it would, after hours and hours of knitting.

The second reason to knit a swatch is to determine gauge, a process that can bring veteran knitters to their knees. Fortunately, in lace knitting, strict adherence to gauge is not critical for every project, but it still will provide you with information to help you block your finished work properly. In Part 3 of this book, a gauge is stated for each project.

tip: Often, knitting charts show only the right side of the work (odd-numbered rows). If this is the case, the pattern will tell you how to work all wrong-side (even-numbered) rows; usually, you will simply knit the knit stitches and purl the purl stitches.

For the fitted garments, such as the Vintage Kneesocks (page 107) and the Deirdre Sweater (page 132), the blocked, finished gauge and dimensions are given; just as for any other type of knitting, achieving the correct gauge is crucial for a properly fitted finished garment. However, for the shawls, scarves, and wraps, which do not require exact gauge, unblocked gauge is given, and both the unblocked and blocked dimensions of the finished piece are included. It is much easier to check your unblocked gauge for these types of projects because the blocked gauge depends to some extent on how much you stretch the piece.

BLOCKING LACE

When you cast off the last stitch of your lace project, your project is not yet done. Lace almost always needs to be blocked to open up the design and allow all those beautiful airy patterns to show in their true glory. Blocking also smoothes out any slight variations and irregularities in your knitting, allowing you to achieve a professional finish. Don't skip this step!

At its most basic, blocking refers to wetting a piece of knitting; placing it on a flat surface; stretching, pushing, or pulling it into the desired final shape; and allowing it to dry. The three main methods of blocking are wet blocking, steam blocking, and spray blocking.

wet blocking

For the most airy lace, like dainty shawls and garments that consist mostly of openwork, I like to use a wet-blocking technique because it allows the stitches to open up as much as possible.

To wet block, fill your sink with warm water and pour in a tablespoon or so of wool wash or a small squirt of shampoo. If your project is knit in an animal fiber that you want to soften, such as wool, add a small amount of hair conditioner to the water. Soak the knitted piece in the water for about fifteen minutes. You may swish it around gently, but remember that unless they are labeled *superwash*, many fibers will felt with too much agitation in warm water. Rinse the piece in clear water of the same temperature, roll your piece in a clean towel, and gently blot any excess water.

TOOLS FOR BLOCKING

You don't need much to beautifully block a lace project—just a flat surface you don't mind stabbing with pins and a few other items, like blocking wires. You can purchase T-pins and blocking wires at most knitting and craft retail outlets.

BLOCKING SURFACE I do most of my blocking on my living room carpet or on flat foam squares. These squares are convenient, portable, and can be put together and pulled apart like puzzle pieces to fit any size project. (They are sold as exercise mats or play mats for children and can be found online and in brick-and-mortar retail outlets.) But pretty much any surface that has a bit of cushioning that you can push a pin into will work—so get creative!

PINS Rustproof T-pins are a must to hold the stretched piece of lace in place until it dries. Keep at least a hundred T-pins on hand in a container with a tight-fitting lid. (I do, yet still I manage to tip over my box of T-pins at least once a year.)

BLOCKING WIRES Blocking wires are long, thin, flexible wires that you can thread through the straight edges of your lace piece and pin into place using your trusty T-pins. Good places to use blocking wires? The long straight top edge and center back of a triangular shawl and the straight edges inside a shawl's pointed edging.

TAPE MEASURE OR YARDSTICK A tape measure or a yardstick will help ensure that you are not only blocking your piece to the appropriate size but also blocking evenly.

SPRAY BOTTLE Once dry, a blocked piece will retain its pinned shape. If you want to make adjustments after the piece has dried, use a spray bottle of water to dampen the area you want to reblock, then pin the piece as desired.

Spread the piece out on a dry, clean blocking surface like a carpet or a bed covered with a fresh sheet or duvet. Stretch the piece as needed to achieve the finished measurements and shape indicated in the pattern. Use rustproof T-pins and/or blocking wires to hold the knitted piece in place, and let it dry completely. After it is completely dry, unpin your piece. It will retain the shape that you gave it. Be aware that you may get a little "bounce back" if you have really stretched your piece to the limit, so your finished size may be slightly smaller.

steam blocking

To steam block an item, you use, not surprisingly, a steam iron or a steamer. You will achieve best results with an iron that has a good powerful "shot of steam" function. I like to steam block items that don't need a lot of stretching, for example, the Lace Stripe Scarf (page 40). It is best not to use this method on synthetic fibers, however, because the heat and steam could melt the fibers and destroy your knitting.

Many techniques can be used for shaping your piece when steam blocking. You can stretch and pin your work before steaming, after steaming, or simply pull the piece into shape with your fingers as you steam—of course, being careful not to steam your fingers in the process.

I find that wool stands up nicely to a lot of heat and steam, which I apply directly to the knitted piece. I am more gentle with silk, using a lower heat setting and barely touching the surface of the iron to the piece. If you are unsure how steam blocking will affect your fabric, place a damp cloth between your knitting and the steam as protection, or experiment on a swatch before blocking the finished piece.

spray blocking

Spray blocking is the most gentle blocking process and should be used with delicate and costly fibers, like cashmere or qiviut, and with fibers of unknown origin.

Pin your piece to the desired dimensions, and lightly spray it with water from a spray bottle. Make sure you get it damp enough to relax the fibers, but don't soak it. Let the piece dry completely before unpinning.

THE LACE KNITTER'S FIX-IT TOOLKIT

While learning to knit lace is not too difficult, it has its pitfalls. Errors can be difficult to spot and fix. Stitches that accidentally slip off the needles are prone to unravel, making it nearly impossible to pick them up and repair them. Fortunately, a few simple tools—and tips and tricks you can learn—will make your lace-knitting experience pleasant and successful.

stitch markers

The big advantage of stitch markers is that using them makes it much easier to catch errors, particularly if you are new to lace. Slip plastic, rubber, or metal rings (or even knotted loops of waste yarn) onto your needle to mark the beginning of a round or to signify a change in pattern (for example, from a background to a charted pattern, or between charted patterns) or pattern repeats. With markers, you control the number of stitches that you need to monitor at any one time, regardless of how many total stitches are on your needle. When you get to a marker in your knitting, simply slip it from your left-hand needle to your right-hand needle, then work the next stitch.

Stitch markers can slow you down somewhat because you have to slip every marker as you encounter it. If you are knitting a piece 100 stitches wide, for example, and your pattern repeat is 4 stitches, that's a lot of marker-slipping! In such a case, you might place a marker every second or third repeat and still find them helpful for minimizing the possibility of error.

Of course, lace often involves decreases of 2 or 3 stitches at a time, and if a pattern repeat starts and ends in the middle of such a maneuver, you'll have a stitch marker to fiddle with in addition to your decrease. Avoid getting stuck midmaneuver by planning ahead. Take a look at the sample chart at right.

The 10-stitch pattern repeat is denoted with dotted lines. Let's say that your piece is 35 stitches around. For each round, the pattern would direct you to work the first 2 stitches of the chart, work the 10-stitch repeat 3 times (for a total of 30 stitches worked), and then work the last 3 stitches of the chart.

On chart rounds 3 and 5, the repeat begins with 1 double decrease and 1 yarn over; the remaining yarn over is at the end of the repeat. If you had placed stitch markers to mark the pattern repeats, you would have done so after stitches 2, 12, 22, and 32. For round 3, you would work the first 2 stitches as knit 1 and yarn over, but 1 stitch would remain on the needle before your 1st stitch marker.

To maintain the proper number of stitches in your repeat, you would have to slip the next stitch, unworked, from the left-hand needle to the right-hand needle, remove the marker, slip the unworked stitch back to the left-hand needle, and replace the marker. Then you could work the double decrease and continue the pattern. At the end of the repeat, though, you would have the same situation, because 1 stitch would remain on the left-hand

Stitch Marker Sample Chart

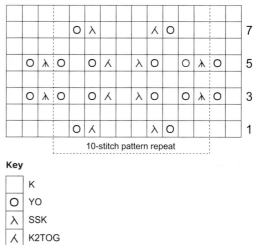

10-stitch pattern repeat

Key

	K
O	YO
λ	SSK
⅄	K2TOG
⋏	SL1 K2TOG PSSO

needle before the marker because you would have added 1 stitch with the yarn over. You would need to move that stitch to the other side of the marker so it could become part of the double decrease that immediately follows the marker.

So much slipping and moving of markers can be tiresome and slow down your knitting progress. Instead, as you work rounds 2 and 4, move the markers 1 stitch to the right. Planning ahead in this way will ensure that the markers will be in the proper position when you work rounds 3 and 5.

lifelines

Lace is notorious for unraveling quickly and with little provocation. How disheartening it can be to discover an error in your lace, begin to rip back several rows to fix it, then suddenly notice your stitches disappearing at an alarming rate. Another extremely frightening scenario: Your knitting accidentally slips off of the needle, and you watch in horror as your hard work unravels as soon as you touch it, if not before. Such are the nightmares of the lace knitter. Lifelines to the rescue!

A lifeline is a length of waste yarn (or thread) that holds a row of stitches in place in the event of unraveling (planned or unplanned). To make a lifeline, cut a piece of waste yarn long enough to extend 4 inches (10cm) or so beyond each end of your row or round, and thread it onto a tapestry needle. Next, *with your work still on the working needle,* slip the tapestry needle under each stitch on the needle as though you were transferring those stitches to waste yarn, but *do not slip the stitches off the working needle.* Also be careful not to thread the lifeline through any stitch markers, and make sure that the working needle doesn't slip out while you are inserting the lifeline.

tip Veteran lace knitters often use dental floss as knitting lifelines because it is strong and slips easily through the stitches.

Continue knitting, leaving the waste yarn threaded through the stitches, taking care not to accidentally knit the lifeline together with your yarn.

Later, if you find an error in your pattern above a lifeline, you can easily rip back to that row and find your stitches intact on the lifeline. Then slip your stitches back onto your working needle and rework that section.

simple stitch solutions

Frequent yarn overs and decreases can be easy to miss here and there in a lace pattern. The good news is that lace mistakes are easy to fix, if you remain vigilant while you knit.

Most of the lace patterns in this book alternate pattern rows with plain "resting" rows, which give you a chance to check your stitch counts and hopefully catch errors before you get too far away from them. If you have used stitch markers between pattern repeats, count your stitches between markers as you work the plain rows to make sure that each pattern repeat has the right number of stitches.

fixing a missed yarn over

If you missed a yarn over (page 32), pick up the yarn from the previous row with the tip of your needle to create the missing yarn over. While this yarn over might be slightly tighter than the others, your piece will even itself out after finishing and blocking.

In the following example, a yarn over is missing after a double decrease. (a)

As you work back on the wrong side, simply pick up the yarn between the last stitch before the decrease and the decrease itself to make the yarn over. To ensure that the stitch is placed on your needle properly, lift up the yarn with your right-hand needle, from the back, or from right to left, and place it on the left-hand needle. (b)

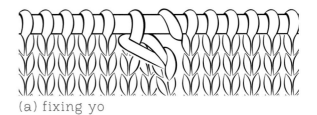

(a) fixing yo

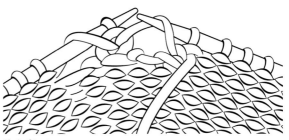

(b) fixing yo

KNIT IN THE KNOW:
LACE KNITTING VS. KNITTED LACE

Lace knitting, knitted lace: What's the difference?

According to some experts, "lace knitting" has patterning on every other row (with a "resting row" in between) and "knitted lace" has patterning on every row. As far as I'm concerned, lace by any name is fabulous!

fixing a missed decrease

If you are knitting a piece that has lace patterning on the right side only and discover a missed decrease in the previous pattern row, you can fix your error without having to rip out the whole row by "dropping" (unraveling in a column) stitches down to the mistake, then working back up to the current row.

For example, assume that you have just noticed that you missed a "knit 2 together, yarn over" combination 2 rows earlier in your work. Work across the row (or round) to just before the stitches above where you missed the decrease, and insert the tip of your right-hand needle into the fronts of the 2 stitches on the row where the decrease should have been made. (c)

Next, drop down to the 2 stitches that should have been "knit 2 together, yarn over" by slipping 2 stitches off the left-hand needle and gently unraveling to the stitches that you slipped onto your right-hand needle. (d)

Slip the 2 stitches that should have been "knit 2 together, yarn over" onto the left-hand needle. Work the decrease (knit 2 together), wrapping with the loose yarn from the bottommost row that you unraveled to complete the stitch. (e)

Still using that loose yarn, work the yarn over as explained in the previous section. Slip the 2 stitches just worked back onto the left-hand needle. (f)

Knit those 2 stitches normally using the loose yarn from the topmost row you unraveled. (g)

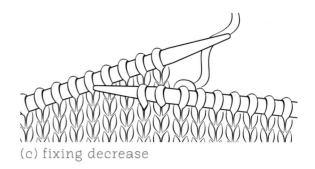

(c) fixing decrease

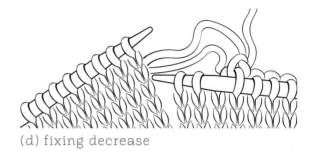

(d) fixing decrease

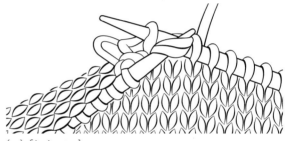

(e) fixing decrease

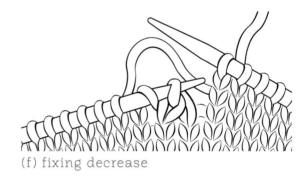

(f) fixing decrease

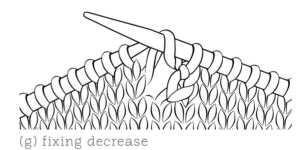

(g) fixing decrease

— PART 2 —

LEARNING
LACE TECHNIQUES

Believe it or not, if you can knit and purl, you can create beautiful lacework. Delicate lace patterns are created by simply working combinations of increases and decreases among the well-known knit and purl stitches.

In this section, you'll learn basic techniques for casting on, joining yarns, and binding off that are particularly well suited for lace as well as a few special cast-ons needed for some of the projects in this book. You'll also find step-by-step instructions for all of the increases and decreases you will need to know to complete the lace projects in this book.

CASTING ON

Different lace projects need different cast-ons, and I've included instructions for the methods used in this book. Which cast-on method is best for a particular lace project depends on how the piece will be constructed—top down, bottom up, or center out, for example. When appropriate, the patterns will tell you which cast-on works best for each project. If a project's instructions do not specify a particular cast-on method, use your favorite. When working a cast-on for lace, remember that lace projects need stretch so they can be blocked to their full beauty. Take a look at the techniques that follow for getting some stitches on your needles.

provisional cast-on

The Provisional Cast-On is used when you want the beginning of your work to have "live" stitches later—that is, stitches that you will pick up and work in the opposite direction or graft to another set of live stitches to complete a piece. The True Love Scarf or Stole pattern (page 50) uses this technique.

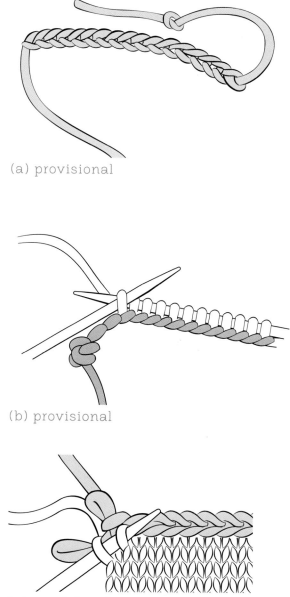

(a) provisional

Using a smooth waste yarn in a color that contrasts with and is approximately the same weight as your working yarn, crochet a chain that is several stitches longer than the number of stitches you need to cast on. Cut the yarn (leaving a short tail), pull the tail through the last stitch, and tie a knot in this yarn tail. (At some point in your pattern, you will be directed to "unzip" the provisional cast-on chain and slip the newly live stitches onto a needle; this knot will make the correct end of the chain easy to find. (a)

(b) provisional

Look at your chain. One side of it will be smooth and look like a row of Vs; the opposite side will have a bump in the center of each V. On the "bumpy" side, use your working yarn to knit 1 stitch into each bump until you have the number of cast-on stitches specified for your project. (b)

Work the rest of your pattern as directed. When the pattern directs you to remove the Provisional Cast-On, undo the cast-off end of your crocheted chain. Stick the point of your empty knitting needle into the stitch below the 1st cast-on stitch (the last stitch of your crocheted chain, where

(c) provisional

you tied a knot in the yarn tail) and gently pull the chain to begin to "unzip" it (like opening a bag of pet food). Stick the tip of the needle in each successive stitch and slip the newly exposed stitches onto your knitting needle, one at a time, as you proceed. (c)

You now have a set of live stitches on your working needle and can proceed as the pattern directs you.

circular cast-on

When you knit a circular shawl, you will cast on a few stitches at the center and then work in the round, increasing according to your pattern instructions, from the center out. There are several different ways to do this, but the Circular Cast-On is my favorite and, in my opinion, the easiest. The Vortex Spiral Shawl or Afghan (page 74) starts with this cast-on.

Using a long-tail cast-on, cast on the number of stitches required over double-pointed needles. For example, if your pattern directs you to cast on 9 stitches, cast on 3 stitches to each of 3 needles. (d)

Join, being careful not to twist your stitches, and with a fourth double-pointed needle work your 1st round. Use a safety pin (or waste yarn) to keep track of the beginning of the round. (e)

Follow the pattern instructions. When you have increased to a number of stitches that spread out easily on your shortest circular needle, transfer your work to that circular needle to continue working in the round. Replace the safety pin with a stitch marker to mark the beginning of the round. (f)

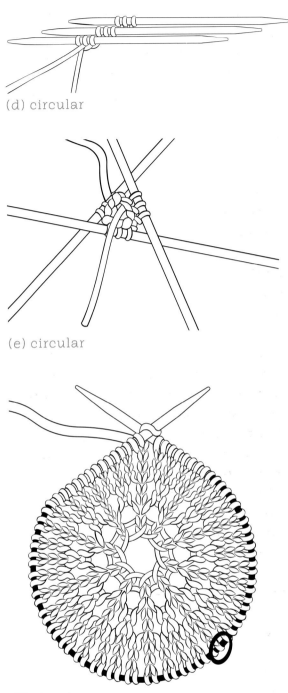

(d) circular

(e) circular

(f) circular

KNIT IN THE KNOW:
CIRCULAR CAST-ON TIPS

Some knitters find a circular cast-on difficult because of the relatively few number of stitches per needle at the beginning. Ease your cast-on woes with the following tricks:

Cast on all your stitches to 1 double-pointed needle and work 1 row across the stitches. Turn your work, divide the stitches over 3 double-pointed needles, and join the stitches to knit in the round.

Use short double-pointed needles; a 4-inch (10cm) length (usually marketed as glove needles) is perfect for this technique.

Wooden double-pointed needles may be easier to use than metal, because the stitches will be less likely to slide off a wooden surface.

lace cast-on

You will need a stretchy edge for your lace projects, and the Lace Cast-On is my go-to cast-on for ultimate stretch. If you are casting on for a piece that you plan to block as far as the yarn will let you, such as the Lace Stripe Scarf (page 40), the Cranbourne Scarf (page 46), Elizabeth's Cowl (page 43), or the Light-as-a-Feather Smoke Ring (page 120), use this technique.

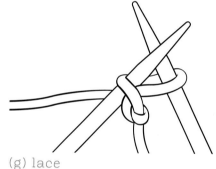

(g) lace

Make a slip knot, and place it on the left-hand needle. Put the tip of the right-hand needle through the *back* of the slip knot. Wrap the working yarn around the needle and pull it through. (g)

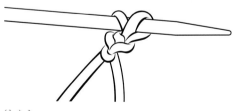

(h) lace

Slip the new loop from the right-hand needle onto the left-hand needle without twisting it. (h)

Continue to cast on stitches by putting the tip of the right-hand needle into the *front* of each loop, wrapping the working yarn around the needle, pulling it through, and placing the new loop onto the left-hand needle without twisting. (The new stitches are created as if knitting. No wonder this technique also is known as "knitting on"!) (i)

easy garter stitch tab

This easy technique builds upon the backward loop cast-on for a quick start to a triangular shawl worked from the top down (that is, knit from the center back of the neck down), increasing as you go. Use the Easy Garter Stitch Tab for the Stacy Shawl (page 58) and the Two-Thirds Shawl (page 64).

Using the backward loop cast-on, cast on 3 stitches (or the number specified in your pattern). (j)

Knit 8 rows, or the number specified in your pattern. (k)

Pick up and knit 1 stitch from each garter stitch ridge along the long edge of the strip you have just knit. (For 8 rows, you would have 4 ridges.) (l)

Pick up and knit the stitches along the cast-on edge. (In this example, 3 cast-on stitches; you would have a total of 10 stitches on your needles.) You are ready to start working your pattern. (m)

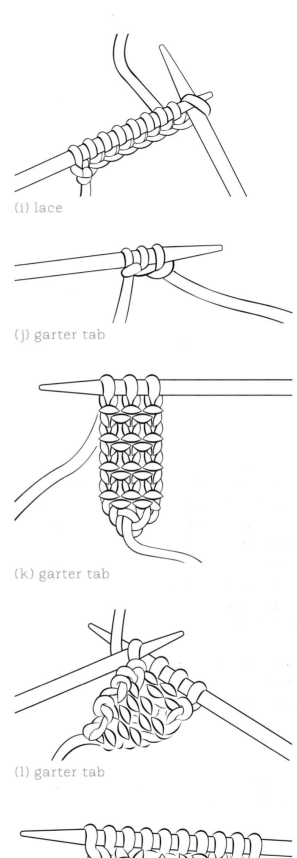

(i) lace

(j) garter tab

(k) garter tab

(l) garter tab

(m) garter tab

picked-up stitches

Sometimes a lace project will use the edge of a border pattern as the "cast-on" edge for the main part of the piece. For such projects, you'll start by casting on stitches and knitting a border sideways, working rows back and forth in a given number of pattern repeats. After completing the border, you will turn your work 90 degrees and pick up stitches along the long straight side of the edging and begin the main lace pattern of the project. This technique is used for the Garden Party Cardigan (page 123).

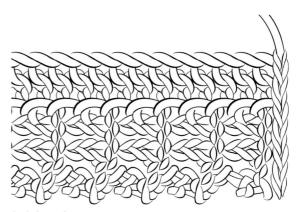

(n) border

Knit your border, working as many repeats as directed by the pattern. Generally, when you knit a border, you will slip the 1st stitch on each row, making a series of loops along the straight edge that will make picking up stitches a breeze. Bind off but do not break the working yarn. (n)

Using the working yarn, pick up and knit 1 stitch in each top loop along the border. (o)

The pattern will tell you how many total stitches to pick up and how many stitches to pick up in each loop.

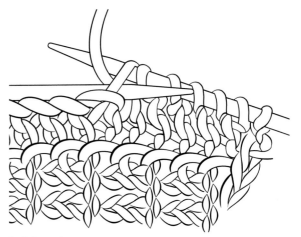

(o) border

TOE-UP CAST-ONS

I think it's important to dedicate as much space as possible in this book to the techniques you'll use in almost every lace project, and so I do not go into detail here on the "family" of cast-ons used for toe-up socks.

For the three sock patterns in this book, there are several toe-up cast-ons that you can use, including Short-Row, Turkish, Figure-Eight, and Judy's Magic Cast-On, all of which you can find documented online. For my complete, step-by-step instructions and to learn more about my favorite methods, refer to my previous books *Socks from the Toe Up* and *Toe-Up Socks for Every Body*.

JOINING YARNS

Unless you happen to be working from a giant skein or cone of yarn that has enough yardage to complete your project, you will have to join a new skein of yarn to the working yarn at some point in your knitting. There are several easy methods for joining yarns in lace projects so that the join is not noticeable.

easy join

This almost invisible join is perfect for use with yarns up to a light sportweight, making it a great choice for lace projects. The Easy Join is my favorite and the one I use most often because it is quick and requires no tools. It is also strong, so you can block your lace as aggressively as you like without any fear of the join coming undone.

When you have no less than 3 inches (7.5cm) of the current yarn remaining, pick up the new yarn and hold it together with the working yarn, leaving a tail of the new yarn about 2 inches (5cm) long. Knit 4 or 5 stitches with both yarns held together. (a)

On the next row (or round): When you come to the stitches that you knit with the 2 strands of yarn in the previous row (or round), *be sure to work both strands* of each stitch. (b)

After working across these stitches, gently pull on the dangling ends to tighten up the first and last stitches of the join. Block the piece, then trim the yarn tails close to the fabric.

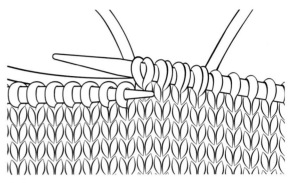

(a) easy join

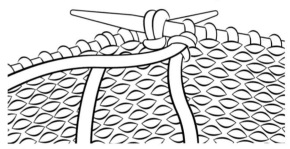

(b) easy join

Russian join

The Russian Join is another effective way to securely join two yarns. Like the Easy Join, it creates an almost invisible join and is very sturdy. I use it with fine yarns because it will add some bulk to your knitting at the point of the join.

Thread a tapestry needle through the end of 1 of the yarns, fold the tail back on the yarn about 2 inches (5cm) and weave the needle in and out of the plies of that same end for 1 or 2 inches (2.5 or 5cm), but do not pull it tight. (c)

Form a loop with the end of the 1st yarn, and insert the end of the 2nd yarn through this loop and pull it through. (d)

Now thread the end of the 2nd yarn through the tapestry needle and weave the needle in and out of the plies of that strand as you did the 1st one. (e)

After you have woven up to the loop, gently pull on both yarns until the loop disappears. Clip the excess yarn. (f)

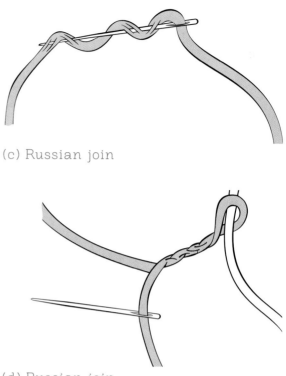

(c) Russian join

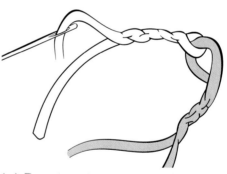

(d) Russian join

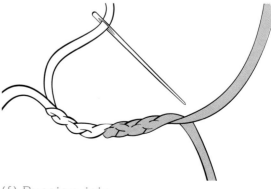

(e) Russian join

(f) Russian join

spliced join

The Spliced Join is usually called, somewhat inelegantly, "spit splicing." This method is appropriate only for animal fibers that will felt when heat, moisture, and agitation are applied. The yarns should have at least two plies. This join works especially well for invisibly joining yarns thicker than sportweight, because it does not double the yarn thickness at the join.

On the ends of the 2 yarns that you mean to splice together, separate and pull apart the plies for about 2 inches (5cm). Spread out the plies a bit to fluff up the fibers. (g)

Overlap the 2 fluffy yarn ends in your hand, tails in opposite directions, and (I apologize in advance) spit on them. Get the ends nice and wet! (You could pour water on the plies, but almost everyone I know who uses this method just spits on the yarn.) Next, rub the yarn back and forth vigorously between your hands to generate the heat and friction needed to felt the fibers together. When you are done, you will have 1 continuous strand of yarn. (h)

A word of caution: Some knitters swear by the Spliced Join and say that it will never come apart; however, I am a bit suspicious and have seen other knitters struggle with it. Perhaps I am not vigorous enough in my spitting or rubbing (or both), but I would not use this method to join yarns in a piece that I planned to block severely. I fear that when I block my lace, the spit-splices will come undone and my lace will be ruined. Proceed with care and at your own risk.

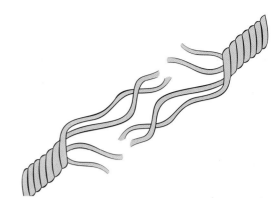

(g) spliced join

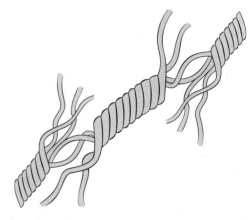

(h) spliced join

BINDING OFF

Because they are blocked (sometimes severely) as part of the finishing process, lace projects require stretchy bound-off and cast-on edges. Two methods are presented here. In general, use the Russian Bind-Off when a pattern directs you to "bind off all stitches loosely," and use the Knitted-On Border technique when a pattern directs you to knit an edging onto the "live" stitches of the body of the piece.

Russian bind-off

The Russian Bind-Off is a favorite of mine because it is quick and easy and produces a nicely stretchy edge. In fact, this is the only bind-off I use for shawls that are finished by binding off many stitches across the longest or widest edge, such as the Tiffany Triangle Shawl (page 68) and the Two-Thirds Shawl (page 64). To make sure the bound-off edge is stretchy enough to let you block your piece to its limits (so the lace can realize its full potential), work the Russian Bind-Off with a needle one or two sizes larger than the needle used to knit the piece.

Knit 2, slip these 2 stitches back to the left-hand needle, and knit these 2 stitches together through the back loops. (a)

Knit 1, slip the 2 stitches on the right-hand needle back to the left-hand needle, and knit 2 together. (b)

Repeat the previous step until 1 stitch remains. Cut your yarn and pull the end through the last loop. (c)

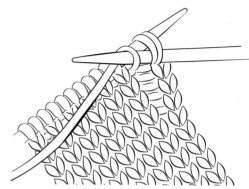

(a) Russian bind-off

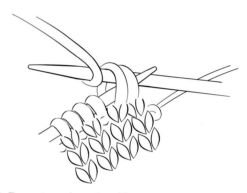

(b) Russian bind-off

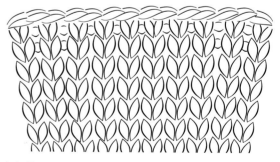

(c) Russian bind-off

knitted-on border

For a project with a border, some knitters knit the border separately and then sew it onto the bound-off edges of the body of the piece. I find it much more gratifying to knit a border directly onto a lace piece for two reasons: I don't have to do any sewing, and (more important) a knitted-on border will be more elastic than a sewn-on one.

Some projects have a border all the way around the piece, such as the Vortex Spiral Shawl or Afghan (page 74), and the ends of the border need to be joined together somehow. You may use either the Provisional Cast-On (which requires you to graft together the border ends) or your favorite cast-on, (which requires you to sew the border's bound-off edge to the cast-on edge).

Begin by casting on the number of border stitches for your pattern, using the working yarn that is still attached to the last stitch of the main piece of your project. Then knit as many repeats of the border pattern as needed to "use up" all the live stitches from the edge of the main piece. Because the border is worked back and forth (perpendicular to the edge of the main piece), you will attach the border to the main piece only on every other row, knitting 2 rows of border for every live stitch along the edge of the main piece.

The following example starts by casting on (using the Lace Cast-On) 7 stitches with the working yarn at the end of this last row of the main piece, with the right side of the work facing. (d)

Turn the work. Knit to 1 stitch before the end, then knit the last stitch together with 1 stitch from the edge of the shawl. (e)

Turn the work. Slip 1 stitch purlwise with the yarn in front, then work the 1st row of the border pattern. (f)
Note: On this and all odd-numbered rows, slip the 1st stitch purlwise with the yarn in front.

Turn the work. Work the 2nd row of the border pattern to the 2nd to last stitch, then knit the last stitch of the chart together with 1 stitch along the edge of the main piece. (g)
Note: On this and all even-numbered rows, knit the last stitch together with 1 stitch along the edge of the main piece.

When you have knit all the stitches along the edge of the main piece, bind off the border loosely.

tip You can also use the Knitted-On Border technique to add a border to a bound-off edge. Just knit the last stitch of the border pattern together with a bound-off stitch along the edge of the main piece.

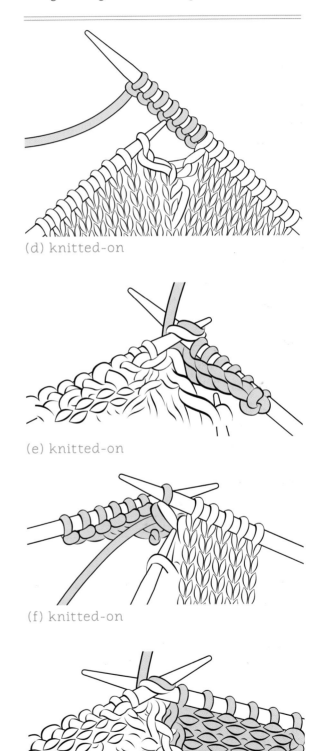

(d) knitted-on

(e) knitted-on

(f) knitted-on

(g) knitted-on

MAKING INCREASES

If you are going to knit lace, you are going to make increases by working yarn overs. The humble Yarn Over might be considered the most basic of all lace stitches, and I love that, when combined with decreases, this simple stitch forms even the most intricate of lace patterns. The importance of executing a yarn over properly in lace cannot be overstated and, I believe, makes an in-depth look at the technique worthwhile.

yarn over (yo)

The Yarn Over (abbreviated "yo") is integral to what makes lace, well, lacy. It's the easiest way to add an increase and make a hole in your knitting: Simply wrap the working yarn around your needle. Unless you are using a yarn over to deliberately make an extra stitch, you will pair it with some sort of decrease to maintain the same number of stitches in each row.

Although *yarn over* is a generic term, the technique can be worked in many ways. Just keep in mind that the working yarn should begin between the needles at the front of the piece, whether you are working knit or purl stitches. When you come to a yarn over you created on the previous row, it will not look like the rest of the stitches because it's not "growing" out of the stitch directly below it. Instead, the back leg grows out of the stitch below

it and to the left, and the front leg of the yarn over grows out of the stitch below it and to the right. Despite its different appearance, however, the yarn over stitch should be worked exactly like any other stitch.

The following paragraphs explain how to work yarn overs for the projects in this book.

yarn forward (yfwd)

This yarn over is worked between 2 knit stitches. Complete the 1st knit stitch; the working yarn is at the back of your work. Bring the yarn forward between the needles as if to purl. Before you work the next knit stitch, wrap the yarn over the top of the needle so that it is back in the proper position to knit. (a)

Knit the next stitch. (b)

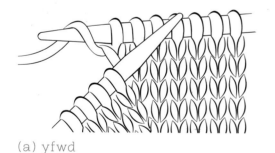

(a) yfwd

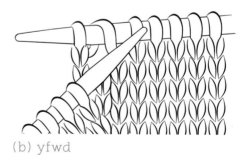

(b) yfwd

yarn round needle (yrn)

This yarn over is worked between 2 purl stitches. Complete the 1st purl stitch; the working yarn is at the front of your work. Wrap the yarn all the way around the needle until it's at the front again. (c)

Purl the next stitch. (d)

double yarn over (double yo)

As the name suggests, the Double Yarn Over creates a hole in a lace pattern double the size of the more common (single) yarn over. Unless you are using a double yarn over to increase the number of stitches in the pattern (a somewhat rare case), it will be paired with 2 decreases (2 single decreases or 1 double decrease).

Wrap the yarn twice around the needle. (e)

Continue to work the pattern. As you work the next row, you will come to the Double Yarn Over you created on the previous row; knit the 1st yarn over and purl the 2nd yarn over. (Alternatively, your pattern may direct you to purl the 1st yarn over and knit the 2nd.) (f)

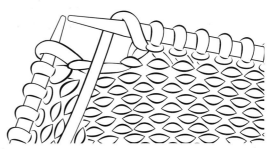

(c) yrn

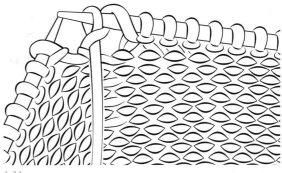

(d) yrn

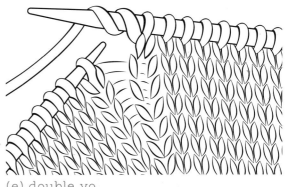

(e) double yo

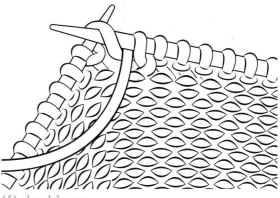

(f) double yo

MAKING SINGLE DECREASES

A yarn over usually is paired with some sort of decrease—1 decrease for each yarn over. In lace, there are many ways to decrease 1 stitch, and each has its own reasons for use, depending on whether the decrease should slant to the left or to the right and whether you are knitting or purling.

knit 2 together (k2tog), right slanting

Knitting 2 stitches together is the only way I know to work a right-slanting single decrease on the right (knit) side of stockinette stitch. And, true to the name, you knit together 2 adjacent stitches as if they were 1 stitch.

Insert the tip of your right-hand needle from left to right through the fronts of the next 2 stitches on the left-hand needle, and wrap the working yarn around the right-hand needle as if you were knitting 1 stitch. (a)

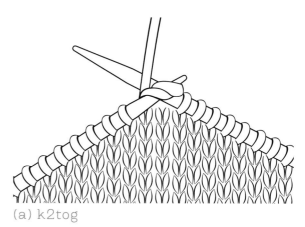

(a) k2tog

Pull the working yarn through and let both stitches slide off the left-hand needle, making 1 knit stitch out of 2. (b)

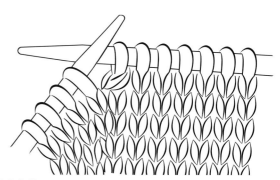

(b) k2tog

purl 2 together (p2tog), right slanting

When working on the wrong (purl) side of stockinette stitch, you can purl 2 stitches together to make a right-slanting single decrease. When viewed from the right side, the decrease looks the same as the Knit 2 Together, which is worked from the right side.

Insert the tip of your right-hand needle from right to left through the fronts of the next 2 stitches on the left-hand needle, and wrap the working yarn around the right-hand needle as if you were purling 1 stitch. (c)

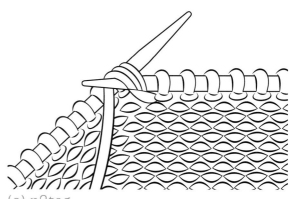

(c) p2tog

Pull the working yarn through and let both stitches slide off the left-hand needle, making 1 stitch out of 2. (d)

slip, slip, knit (ssk), left slanting

The Slip, Slip, Knit creates a left-slanting decrease on the right (knit) side of the work. Traditionally, you would simply slip the first and second stitches as if to knit, and then knit those 2 stitches together. However, I think this method can be improved upon—resulting in an even flatter decrease, and thus lacework that lies even more smoothly.

Slip 1 as to knit. (e)

Slip 1 as to purl. (f)

Knit those 2 stitches together through the back loops. (g)

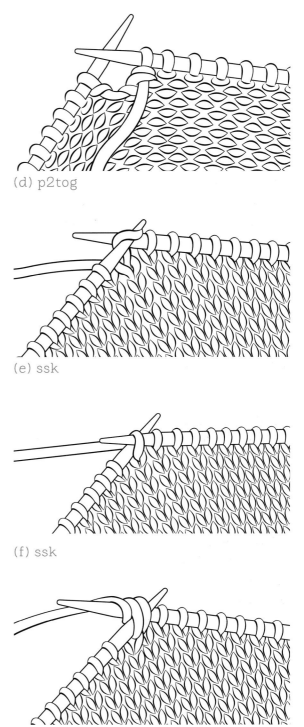

(d) p2tog

(e) ssk

(f) ssk

(g) ssk

knit 2 together through back loops (k2tog tbl), left slanting

Knitting 2 stitches together through the back loops is the fastest way to achieve a left-slanting decrease.

Insert the tip of the right-hand needle from right to left through the back loops of the next 2 stitches on the left-hand needle, and wrap the yarn around the needle as if to knit. (h)

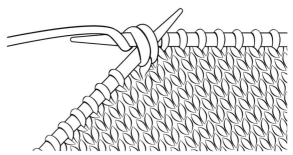

(h) k2tog tbl

Pull the yarn through, and let the 2 stitches slide off of the left-hand needle. (i)

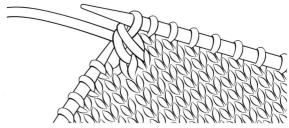

(i) k2tog tbl

purl 2 together through back loops (p2tog tbl), left slanting

There are not many options for working a left-slanting decrease on the wrong (purl) side of stockinette stitch; the Purl 2 Together Through Back Loops works best for me.

Insert the tip of the right-hand needle from left to right (that is, starting with the loop farthest from the working end of your needle) into the back loops of the next 2 stitches on the left-hand needle. (j)

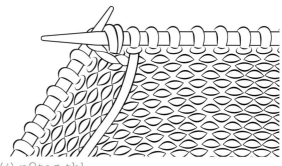

(j) p2tog tbl

Purl the 2 stitches together. (k)

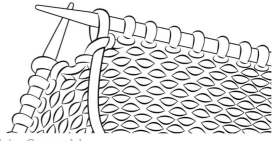

(k) p2tog tbl

MAKING DOUBLE DECREASES

In some of the patterns in this book, you are instructed to work double decreases. A double decrease is a maneuver that decreases 3 stitches to 1 stitch. It generally is paired with 2 yarn overs—1 on each side of the double decrease. As for single decreases, different ways of working double decreases will make your decrease slant to the left or to the right. However, I use only nonslanting double decreases for the projects in this book.

slip 1, knit 2 together, pass slipped stitch over (sl1, k2tog, psso), nonslanting

The following maneuver creates a double decrease on the right (knit) side of your work.

Slip 1 stitch from the left-hand needle to the right-hand needle as if to knit. (a)

Knit the next 2 stitches together, then pass the slipped stitch over the stitch you just knit. (b)

The finished stitch will look a bit like a triangle, with the loops from the 2 outer stitches lying over the center stitch of the old row. (c)

slanting double decreases

As you explore lace further, you may need to work double decreases that slant to the right and to the left, such as knit 3 together (k3tog), purl 3 together (p3tog), slip, slip, slip, knit (sssk), and purl 3 together through the back loop (p3tog tbl). These maneuvers are worked like their single decrease counterparts, but working 3 stitches instead of 2 at a time.

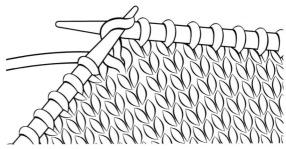

(a) sl1, k2tog, psso

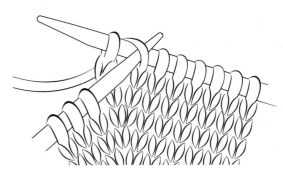

(b) sl1, k2tog, psso

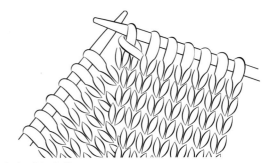

(c) sl1, k2tog, psso

PART 3

KNITTING LACE FOR EVERY DAY

This section contains what I consider to be the "meat" of this book: the projects. Knitters of every skill level will find just the right project. These twenty lace patterns will have you covered in lovely lace from hats to socks.

Each pattern lists a suggested skill level. If you are new to knitting—or to lace—you'll probably want to start at the Beginner level with a simple, quick-knit project such as the Lace Stripe Scarf (page 40) or the Rhossili Beach Watch Cap (page 112). An Intermediate knitter should be ready to knit shawls, stoles, and accessories such as the Stacy Shawl (page 58) and Mairi Tam (page 116). An Advanced knitter will find plenty to occupy her needles as well—including my favorite project, the True Love Scarf or Stole (page 50). To make these Advanced projects, a knitter must have some knowledge of shaping and special construction techniques, as well as experience with all the lace techniques in Part 2.

Of course, no two knitters have the same experience, and not every pattern in the same skill level requires the same experience.

LACE STRIPE SCARF

Worked in stripes of garter stitch alternated with a simple lace pattern, this scarf is a fast, fun knit—and the perfect first project for a beginning knitter—or any knitter who wants to try lace for the first time. You don't even need to read a chart! My test knitter for this design, Muriel Correa, is a beginning knitter with just about a year of experience under her needles. She reported to me that this project was easy and enjoyable. Of course, you don't have to be a beginner to love a quick knit. This scarf would make a great last-minute handmade gift. And if you want a longer scarf, buy an extra skein of yarn and just keep knitting!

Skill Level
Beginner

Size
One size

Finished Measurements (excluding fringe)
48" x 10" (122cm x 25.5cm) unblocked, 70" x 10" (178cm x 25.5cm) blocked

Gauge
4 stitches = 1" (2.5cm) unblocked in garter stitch

Needles
US size 8 (5mm), or size needed to attain gauge

Yarn
2 skeins Madelinetosh Tosh DK, 100% superwash Australian merino, 3.2 oz (90g), 225 yd (206m), Lapis (3) DK, Light Worsted

Fringe
Measure and cut 108 pieces of yarn that are each 22" (56cm) long. Set these pieces of yarn aside for the fringe, which you will attach after you finish knitting the scarf.

Scarf
Using the Lace Cast-On, cast on 42 stitches. Work as follows:

Rows 1-6: Knit across.
Rows 7 and 9: K1, [yo, k2tog] to the last stitch, k1.
Rows 8 and 10: K1, [yo, p2tog] to the last stitch, k1.

Repeat rows 1–10 until the scarf measures 48" (122cm) long. Knit 6 rows plain. Bind off loosely. Weave in ends.

Finishing
Steam block or wet block your Scarf to the finished measurements.

attach the fringe
Divide the 108 pieces of yarn into 18 groups of 6 strands each. You will attach 9 groups of fringe to each short end of the scarf (the cast-on and bound-off rows).

To attach fringe to 1 end of the scarf, fold 1 group of 6 yarn strands in half. Using a crochet hook, pull the yarn (at the fold) about 1" (2.5cm) or so through a stitch at 1 corner. Next, pass the ends of the fringe through this loop, and pull the loop tight against the scarf edge. Repeat this process at the other corner of the scarf end.

In the same manner, attach another group of yarn strands halfway between the 2 corners. You now have 3 groups of fringe attached. Attach the remaining 6 groups of yarn strands between the center and the side edges of the scarf, spacing the yarn evenly, for a total of 9 sets of fringe attached. Repeat this process at the other end of the scarf.

ELIZABETH'S COWL

ELIZABETH'S COWL

My sample knitter for this piece, Laura Linneman, gave this cowl its name. She said, "It reminds me so much of something that Elizabeth Zimmermann would make—the sturdy single-ply wool combined with a garter stitch border and a simple lace pattern. It's a cowl to make Elizabeth proud." I hope that Elizabeth, the "grandmother" of modern knitting, would agree. This project is perfect for a brand-new lace knitter because it is knit in a heavier yarn and features a simple lace pattern.

Skill Level
Beginner

Size
One size

Finished Measurements
16½" (42cm) neck circumference (easily adjustable, see Note below), 8" (20.5cm) high (from edge to edge)

Gauge
4¼ stitches = 1" (2.5cm) unblocked in stockinette stitch

Needles
US size 9 (5.5mm) 16" (40cm) circular needle, or size needed to attain gauge

Yarn
Green Mountain Spinnery Mountain Mohair, 30% mohair, 70% wool, 2 oz (56g), 140 yd (128m), Glacier Lake (4) Medium

NOTE: This project is easy to make larger or smaller: Simply cast on more or fewer stitches in groups of 7, then adjust the number of 7-stitch pattern repeats accordingly. Or, use a different-sized yarn and needles. (For example, a chunky or bulky-weight yarn and a needle a couple of sizes larger than stated in the pattern instructions would make a larger cowl.)

Cowl
Cast on 70 stitches using the Lace Cast-On.
Join into a round, being careful not to twist your stitches.
Round 1: Knit around.
Round 2: Purl around.
Repeat rounds 1 and 2 once more.

start the lace pattern
Work row 1 of the 7-stitch Lace Chart 10 times around.
Then work rows 2, 3, and 4. On odd-numbered rounds work the lace pattern and on even-numbered rounds, knit around.
Continue working all 4 rows of the Lace Chart until the piece measures 7½" (19cm) or the desired length from the cast-on edge, ending after completing row 4 of the chart.

Next round: Purl around.

Next round: Knit around.

Repeat rounds 1 and 2 once more.

Bind off loosely knitwise. Weave in ends.

Finishing

Steam block or wet block your Cowl to the finished measurements.

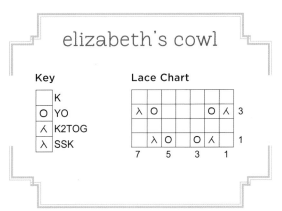

elizabeth's cowl

Key

	K
O	YO
入	K2TOG
λ	SSK

Lace Chart

入	O				O	入	3
	入	O		O	入		1

7　　5　　3　　1

CRANBOURNE SCARF

When I was a child, my family lived for several years in an English village. Our house on Cranbourne Drive had casement windows with many leaded panes of glass. I loved that my bedroom windows had tiny diamond-shaped panes. As a child from the American suburbs, I found these windows exotic and spent hours gazing through them, daydreaming about the world beyond and making up stories of a princess held captive in a medieval tower. This scarf reminds me of those windows, and with it I can take some of my childhood daydreams with me wherever I go.

Skill Level
Adventuresome Beginner

Size
One size

Finished Measurements
68" x 14" (172.5cm x 35.5cm) unblocked, 88" x 16" (223.5cm x 40.5cm) blocked

Gauge
5 stitches = 1" (2.5cm) unblocked in stockinette stitch

Needles
US size 6 (4mm), or size needed to attain gauge

Yarn
2 skeins Madelinetosh Tosh Sock, 100% merino, 4 oz (113g), 395 yd (361m), Ivy (1) Superfine

NOTES: Throughout the pattern, always slip the first stitch of each row as if to purl with the yarn held in back.

The charts show odd-numbered rows only. Work the even-numbered rows as directed in the pattern.

Bottom Border
Using the Lace Cast-On, cast on 59 stitches.

Row 1: Knit across.

Row 2: Sl1 wyib, k to end.

Repeat row 2 six times, for a total of 8 border rows.

Chart A
Row 1: Sl1 wyib, k4 (place marker), work row 1 of Chart A (place marker), k5.

Row 2 (and all even-numbered rows): Sl1 wyib, k4 (slip marker), p49 (slip marker), k5.

Continue working the rest of Chart A (34 rows) in this manner. When Chart A has been completed, start Chart B.

Chart B
Row 1: Sl1 wyib, k4 (slip marker), work row 1 of Chart B (slip marker), k5.

Row 2 (and all even-numbered rows): Sl1 wyib, k4 (slip marker), p49 (slip marker), k5.

Continue working Chart B (12 rows) in this manner.

Repeat Chart B (rows 1–12) 32 times more, for a total of 396 rows worked in the Chart B pattern. When Chart B has been completed, start Chart C.

Chart C

Row 1: Sl1 wyib, k4 (slip marker), work row 1 of Chart C (slip marker), k5.

Row 2 (and all even-numbered rows): Sl1 wyib, k4 (slip marker), p49 (slip marker), k5.

Continue working Chart C (38 rows) in this manner.

Top Border

Sl1 wyib, k to end.

Repeat the previous row 6 more times for a total of 7 border rows.

Bind off loosely. Weave in ends.

Finishing

Steam block or wet block your Scarf to the finished measurements.

tip To make the scarf shorter or longer, work fewer or more repeats of Chart B.

cranbourne scarf

Key

	K on RS, P on WS
O	YO
人	K2TOG
λ	SSK
⋏	SL1 K2TOG PSSO

Chart C

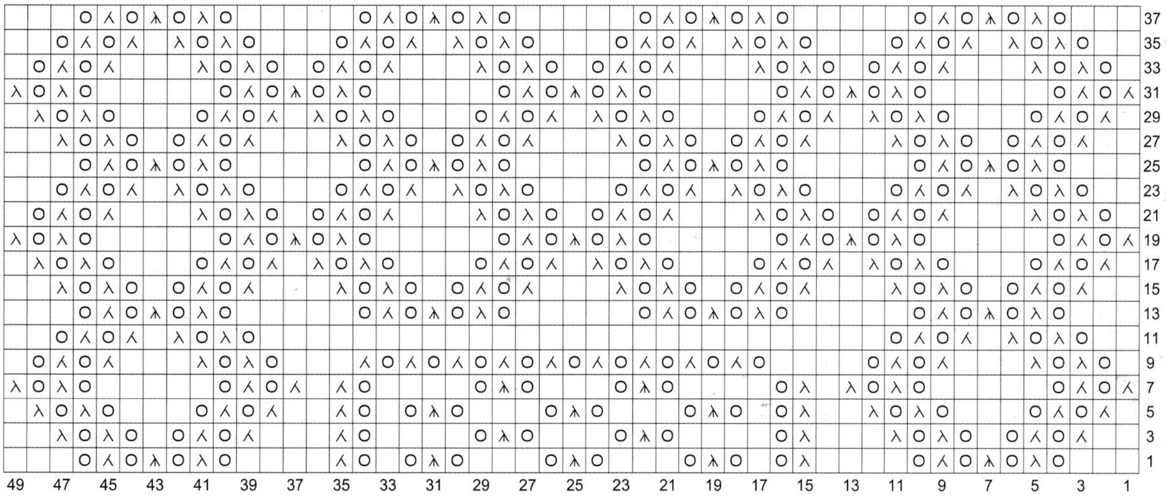

Chart B

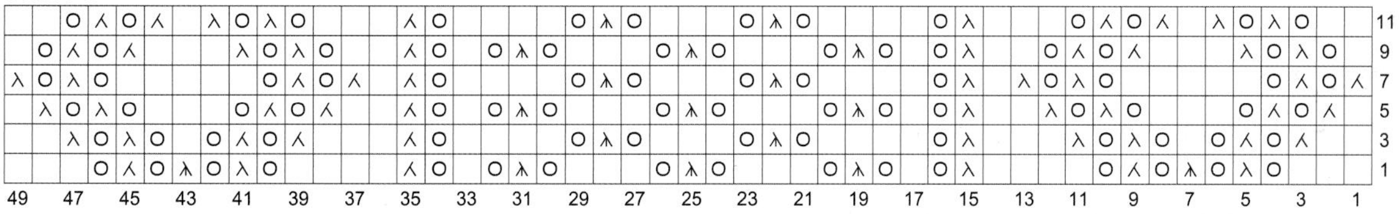

Chart A

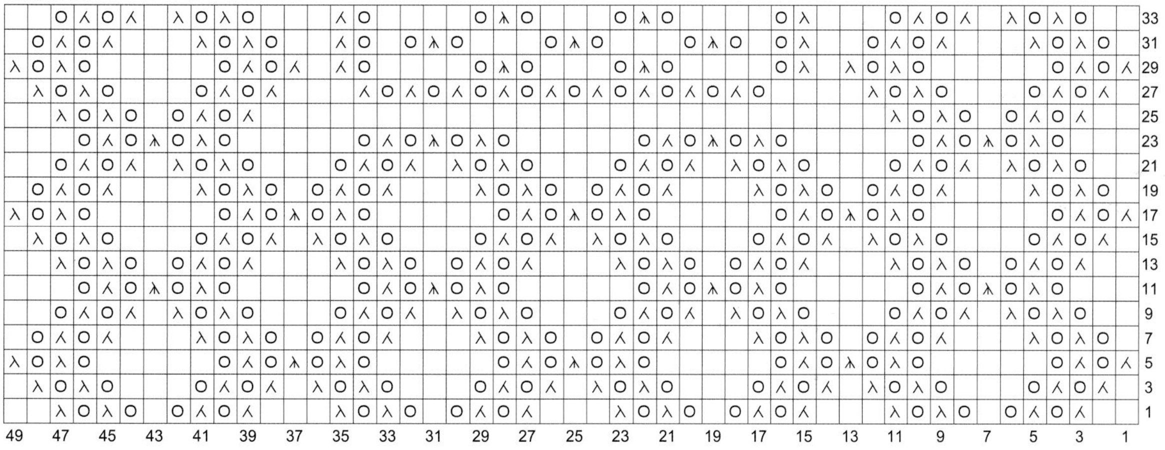

TRUE LOVE SCARF OR STOLE

I call this design "True Love" because knitting it is truly a labor of love. This complex project looks challenging, and it is in some ways, because you must knit the mitered corners and the borders at the same time as the body of the piece. Although the project is a large commitment, none of the stitches are difficult. And I'll tell you a secret: If you find your stitch count is off as you work the mitered corners, just increase or decrease to compensate. No one will ever be able to tell!

Skill Level
Advanced

Size
Two Sizes: Scarf (Stole)

Finished Measurements
SCARF 10" x 40" (25.5cm x 101.5cm) long unblocked, 16" x 60" (40.5cm x 152.5cm) long blocked

STOLE 18" x 50" (45.5cm x 127cm) unblocked 24" x 64" (61cm x 163cm) blocked

Gauge
6 stitches = 1" (2.5cm) unblocked in garter stitch

Needles
US size 4 (3.5mm), or size needed to attain gauge, and 2 double-pointed needles of the same size for grafting

Yarn
SCARF 1 skein Dream in Color Baby, 100% superfine Australian superwash merino, 4 oz (113g), 700 yd (640m), Flamingo Pie (1) Superfine

STOLE 3 skeins Jojoland Cashmere 2-ply, 100% cashmere, 2 oz (56g), 400 yd (366m), Cream (1) Superfine

NOTES: This pattern can be knit in two sizes; just add another repeat of the Center Body Panel Chart C to the basic instructions to transform the Scarf into a Stole.

This pattern is garter stitch lace—you will knit every row. The first set of numbers in the instructions refers to the scarf version, and numbers for the wider stole version immediately follow in parentheses.

The charts show every row: Work the odd-numbered rows right to left and the even-numbered rows left to right, working all single decreases as Knit 2 Together (k2tog) and all double decreases as Slip 1, Knit 2 Together, Pass Slipped Stitch Over (sl1, k2tog, psso).

Bottom Border

Using the Provisional Cast-On, cast on 13 stitches. Knit 1 row.

work the 1st corner

(bottom border chart a)

Row 1: Work across row 1 of Bottom Border Chart A from right to left.

Row 2: Work across row 2 of Bottom Border Chart A from left to right; 2 stitches remain on the right-hand needle. Turn the work.

Row 3: Work right to left as shown on the chart.

Rows 4–9: Continue, working short rows on rows 4, 6, and 8.

Rows 10 and 11: Work across all stitches (22 stitches total).

Rows 12–18: Continue, working the 2nd half of the corner in the same manner as rows 2–8. After row 18, place the stitches on a holder or on a length of waste yarn (14 stitches total).

Undo your provisional cast-on and slip the 13 cast-on stitches onto a needle. Do not knit across these stitches. Using the working yarn from the stitches you have on the holder or waste yarn, and working the chart from left to right, knit the set up row on Bottom Border Chart B.

work across the bottom border

Work Bottom Border Chart B (16 rows) a total of 7 (10) times.

work the 2nd corner

(bottom border chart c)

Work Bottom Border Chart C in the same manner as the 1st corner.

NOTE: At the end of row 9, where you work across all stitches, you will have 21 stitches on the needle at the end of the row.

Work the chart through row 19 (14 stitches remain). Place a marker, and pick up and knit a stitch in each slipped loop along the long straight side of the edging you knit from Bottom Border Chart B—56 (80) stitches picked up. When you reach the stitches on the holder or waste yarn from Bottom Border Chart A, place a marker, then work row 19 of Bottom Border Chart A. Turn the work.

NOTE: In the next row, you will adjust the total number of picked-up stitches. Count your stitches, and if your count is a bit off, figure out how many stitches to increase or decrease in row 20.

Work row 20 of Bottom Border Chart A, then knit across the stitches you picked up, decreasing the number of picked-up stitches to 52 (80). Work the stitches after the next marker as Bottom Border Chart C, row 20.

Body

NOTE: As you work the 1st row of the Body, move the 1st stitch marker 1 stitch to the right (after stitch 11) to mark the end of Body Chart A, and move the 2nd marker 1 stitch to the left (12 stitches from the end) to mark the beginning of Body Chart E.

true love scarf or stole

Key

	K
O	YO
人	K2TOG
U	K1TOG with 1 ST from body
V	SL1 as to P WYIF

Bottom Border Chart A

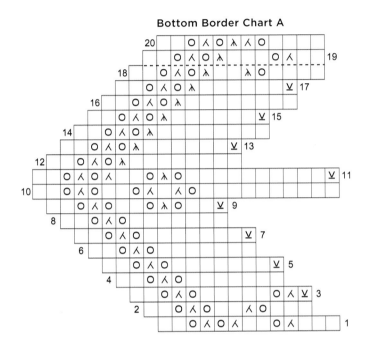

Bottom Border Chart B

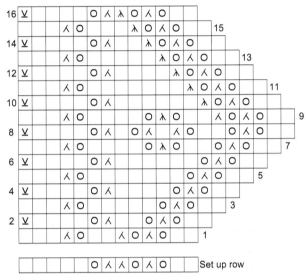

Set up row

Bottom Border Chart C

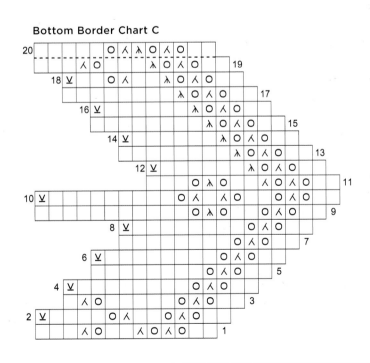

Work across Body Chart A once, work across Body Chart B once, work across Center Body Panel Chart C 1 (2) time(s), work across Body Chart D once, work across Body Chart E once. These 5 charts make up the entire width of the scarf (stole), including the borders on each side of the center panel.

Continue working the 5 charts in this order until each chart (48 rows) has been worked 8 times, removing the two stitch markers as you work across the last row.

Top Border
work the 3rd and 4th corners

Work row 1 of Top Border Chart A (place marker),

true love scarf or stole

Body Chart D

Center Body Panel Chart C

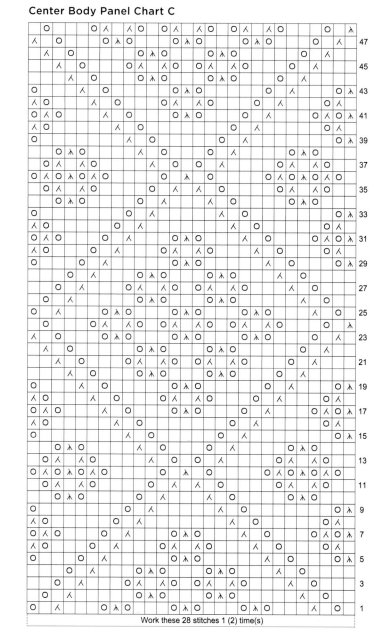

knit across the next 52 (80) body stitches (place marker), work row 1 of Top Border Chart C. Turn the work.

Work row 2 of Top Border Chart C.

Continue to work Top Border Chart C, using short-row shaping as for the 1st and 2nd corners.

Work row 10 of Top Border Chart C, knit across

the 52 (80) body stitches, then work row 2 of Top Border Chart A.

Continue to work Top Border Chart A using short-row shaping.

On row 19, work to the last stitch before the marker. Knit this last stitch together with the 1st stitch after the marker. Turn.

Work row 20, slipping the 1st stitch.

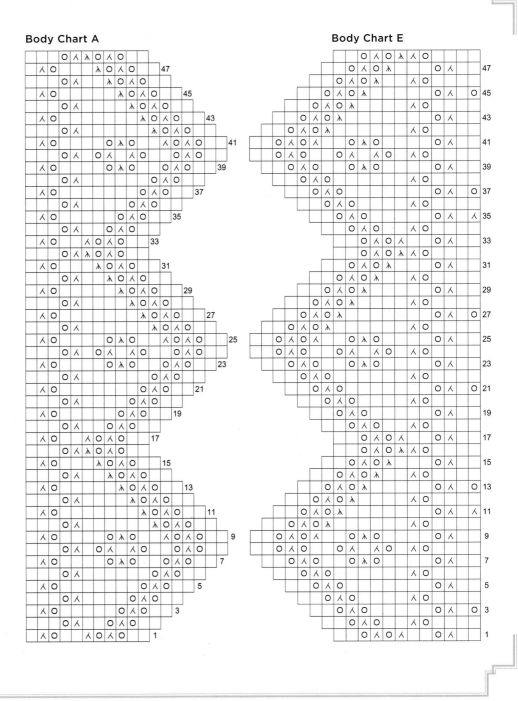

Body Chart B

Body Chart A

Body Chart E

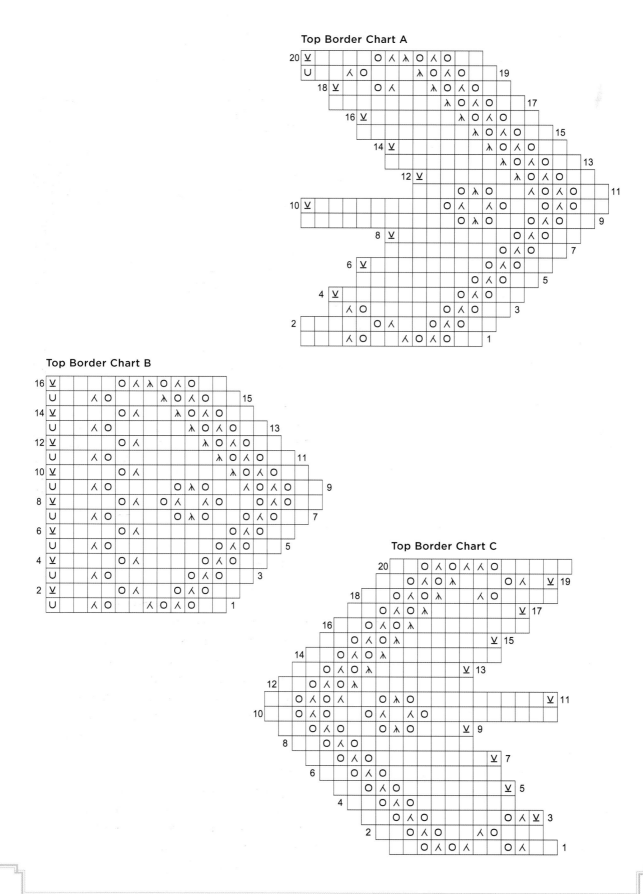

Top Border Chart A

Top Border Chart B

Top Border Chart C

work across the top border

Work Top Border Chart B a total of 7 (10) times, knitting the last stitch on every odd-numbered row together with the next live stitch from the center section. This will work out evenly on the stole stitches.

On the scarf, you have 52 edge stitches attaching to 56 odd-numbered rows, so work an odd row without attaching it to the edge 4 times evenly distributed across the 52 edge stitches.

After completing the 7th (10th) repeat of this chart, work row 1 again, working the last stitch of this row together with the last stitch you attached before the marker. You should have 21 live stitches after the marker.

Put the 13 stitches you just worked on a holder or a length of waste yarn.

work the 4th corner

(top border chart c)

Knit row 11 of Top Border Chart C on the 21 stitches after the marker. Turn the work.

Work rows 12–20, using short-row shaping.

After you complete row 20, you should have 13 stitches on the needle. Put these stitches on 1 double-pointed needle and the 13 stitches from the holder or waste yarn on another double-pointed needle, and graft the edges together. Weave in ends.

Finishing

Steam block or wet block your Scarf or Stole to the finished measurements. Use blocking wires to achieve perfectly straight lines and pins to pull out the points of the edging. Let the piece dry completely before unpinning it.

STACY SHAWL

This shawl is well-rounded, with extra increases worked on the nicely curved front edges so it won't slide off of your shoulders. I originally designed this shawl to showcase a lovely cashmere-blend DK-weight yarn handpainted by my friend Stacy Little of Tempted Yarns, and the pattern was sold as a limited-release kit with that yarn. Because this shawl is knit from a soft wool DK-weight yarn, it is a fairly quick knit and super-snuggly and warm. It is perfect for keeping by your favorite chair where you can easily grab it to wrap around your shoulders on chilly nights.

Skill Level
Intermediate

Size
One size

Finished Measurements
57" (145cm) across the top and 21" (53.5cm) down the center back unblocked, 70" (178cm) across the top and 28" (71cm) down the center back blocked

Gauge
4½ stitches = 1" (2.5cm) unblocked in stockinette stitch

Needles
US size 7 (4.5mm), or size needed to attain gauge

Yarn
2 skeins Dream in Color Classy, 100% superfine Australian superwash merino, 4 oz (113g), 250 yd (229m), Bermuda Teal
[4] Medium

NOTE: To knit 3 in 1 stitch (k3 in 1 st) in this pattern, k1 into the front loop of the next stitch and keep the stitch on the left-hand needle, k1 into the back loop of the same stitch and keep the stitch on the left-hand needle, k1 into the front loop of the stitch again, and finally slide the 3 knitted stitches to the right-hand needle (2 stitches increased).

Easy Garter Stitch Tab
Using a backward loop cast-on, cast on 4 stitches.
Rows 1–15: K2, yo, k2tog. *Do not turn the work after completing row 15.*
Pick up 8 stitches in the 8 ridges along the adjacent long edge and work as follows: K3, yo, k2, yo, k3 (10 new stitches). *Do not turn the work.*
Pick up 4 stitches along the cast-on edge and work as follows: K2, yo, k2tog (4 new stitches; 18 stitches total). Turn the work to begin working from the charts.

A Charts
NOTE: Work across Chart A—Right Side from right to left, then across Chart A—Left Side from right to left. You might find it useful to place stitch markers, as indicated in the instructions for row 1 below, to keep your place.
Row 1 (working from Chart A—Right Side): K2, yo, k2tog (place marker), k3 in 1 st, k3, yo (place marker), k1, (working from Chart A—Left Side) k1 (place marker), yo, k3, k3 in 1 st (place marker), k2, yo, k2tog (24 stitches on the needle). The charts show odd-numbered rows only. Work the even-numbered rows as directed in the pattern.

stacy shawl

Key

☐	K on RS, P on WS
│	K on RS, K on WS
O	YO
⋏	K2TOG
λ	SSK
�🅼	K3 in 1 ST (INC 2 STS)

Chart A—Left Side

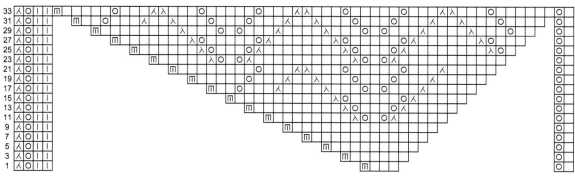

Chart B—Left Side

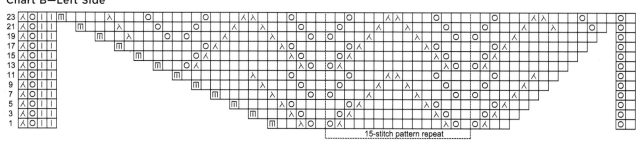

15-stitch pattern repeat

Chart C—Left Side

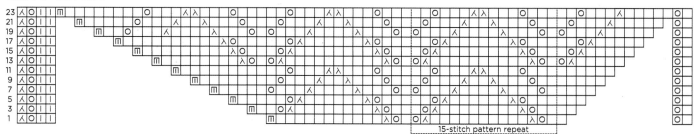

15-stitch pattern repeat

Chart D—Left Side

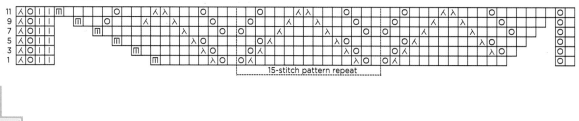

15-stitch pattern repeat

Chart A—Right Side

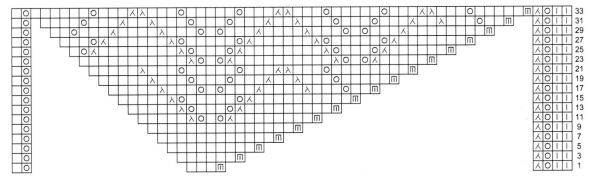

Chart B—Right Side

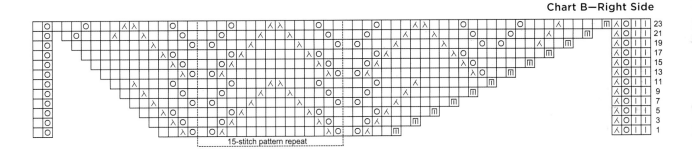

15-stitch pattern repeat

Chart C—Right Side

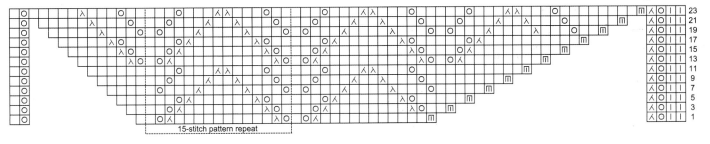

15-stitch pattern repeat

Chart D—Right Side

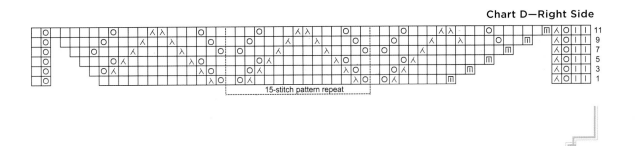

15-stitch pattern repeat

Row 2 (and all even-numbered rows): K2, yo, k2tog, p to the last 4 stitches, k2, yo, k2tog.

Continue in this manner until you have worked all 34 rows of the A charts, working all even-numbered rows as row 2.

B Charts

Work all 24 rows of these charts in the same manner as for the A charts, working right to left across Chart B—Right Side and then Chart B—Left Side.

NOTE: The lace pattern has a 15-stitch repeat, marked by dotted lines. On each B chart, work the stitches before the 1st dotted line, work the 15-stitch pattern repeat 3 times, then work the remaining stitches.

C Charts

Work all 24 rows of the C charts in the same manner as for the previous charts, working right to left across Chart C—Right Side and then Chart C—Left Side.

NOTE: The lace pattern has a 15-stitch repeat marked by dotted lines. On each C chart, work the stitches before the 1st dotted line, work the 15-stitch pattern repeat 5 times, then work the remaining stitches.

D Charts

Work all 12 rows of the D charts in the same manner, working right to left across Chart D—Right Side and then Chart D—Left Side.

NOTE: The lace pattern has a 15-stitch repeat marked by dotted lines. On each D chart, work the stitches before the 1st dotted line, work the 15-stitch pattern repeat 7 times, then work the remaining stitches. Do not break the working yarn.

Edging

Cast on 5 stitches at the end of the last row (a wrong-side row). Turn the work.

Row 1: K2, yo, k2tog, ssk with 1 stitch from the body of the shawl. Turn the work.

Row 2: Slip 1 as to purl, k2, yo, k2tog.

Work these 2 rows across the bottom of the shawl, working 1 shawl stitch together with the Edging on every other row as described in row 1 until you have worked across all the shawl stitches.

Bind off loosely. Weave in ends.

Finishing

Steam block or wet block your Shawl to the finished measurements.

TWO-THIRDS SHAWL

I love creating shawls and stoles in traditional shapes, like triangles and rectangles, but I also like to experiment. This shawl is the result of a shaping experiment: It is two-thirds of a hexagon, consisting of four wedge-shaped sections separated by columns of plain knit stitches. Worked from the top down with increases on each side of each wedge, the shawl grows quickly into a large, lovely piece. Wear it by itself as an outerwear wrap when a coat is too heavy or as a large scarf to add a splash of color and flair over your coat in colder weather.

Skill Level
Adventuresome Intermediate

Size
One size

Finished Measurements
60" (152.5cm) across the top edge and 24" (61cm) down the center back unblocked, 70" (178cm) across the top edge and 30" (76cm) down the center back blocked

Gauge
5 stitches = 1" (2.5cm) unblocked in stockinette stitch

Needles
US size 6 (4mm), or size needed to attain gauge

Yarn
2 skeins Hand Maiden Mini Maiden, 50% silk, 50% wool, 3½ oz (100g), 545 yd (500m), Periwinkle (1) Superfine

NOTE: The Two-Thirds Shawl is worked from charts. Only the odd-numbered rows are charted; on even-numbered rows, work the 3-stitch borders on both ends as specified in the pattern instructions and purl all the stitches in between.

Easy Garter Stitch Tab
Using a backward loop cast-on, cast on 3 stitches. Knit 14 rows.

Next row: K3, pick up and knit 1 stitch in each of the 7 garter ridges along the long edge of the piece, then pick up and knit 1 stitch in each of the 3 cast-on stitches (13 stitches total).

Next row: K3, [yo, k1] 7 times, yo, k3 (21 stitches total).

Next row: K3, p to last 3 stitches, k3.

Next row: K3, yo, k3, yo, k1, yo, k3, yo, k1, yo, k3, yo, k1, yo, k3, yo, k3 (29 stitches total).

Chart A
Row 1 (and all odd-numbered rows): K3, [work the appropriate row from the chart, k1] 3 times, work the appropriate row from the chart, k3 (8 stitches increased per row).

Row 2 (and all even-numbered rows): K3, purl to last 3 stitches, k3.

Work all 40 rows of Chart A in this manner. (After completing Chart A, you will have 45 stitches in each of the 4 pattern repeats and a total of 189 stitches on your needles, including the 3-stitch borders and the 1-stitch dividers that separate the inner "wedges" of the pattern.)

B Charts

Continuing to work the border and divider stitches as set, in each of the 4 wedges, work across Chart B1 once, work across Chart B2 twice, then work across Chart B3 once until all 40 rows of the B charts have been worked. (After completing the B charts, you will have 85 stitches in each of the 4 wedges and a total of 349 stitches on your needles.)

Work the B charts again from the beginning, but this time work across Chart B1 once, work across Chart B2 four times, then work across Chart B3 once until all 40 rows of the B charts have been worked. (After completing the B charts for the 2nd time, you will have 125 stitches in each of the 4 wedges and a total of 509 stitches on your needles.)

two-thirds shawl

Chart A

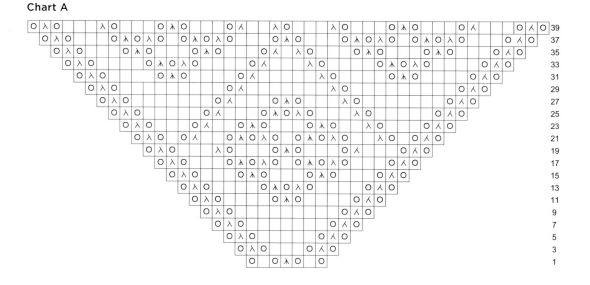

Key

	K on RS, P on WS
O	YO
λ	K2TOG
λ	SSK
ʎ	SL1 K2TOG PSSO

Chart B3

Chart C

Continuing to work the border and divider stitches as set, in each of the 4 wedges, work across Chart C, working the 20-stitch pattern repeat 6 times. Work Chart C in the same manner as charts A and B through row 21. For rows 22, 23, 24 of Chart C, knit across all stitches (while continuing to work the increases on row 23 as shown on the chart), so that you are working these rows in garter stitch.

(After completing Chart C, each of the 4 wedges will have 149 stitches, and you will have a total of 605 stitches on your needles.)
Bind off all stitches loosely using the Russian Bind-Off. Weave in ends.

Finishing

Steam block or wet block your Shawl to the finished measurements.

Chart C

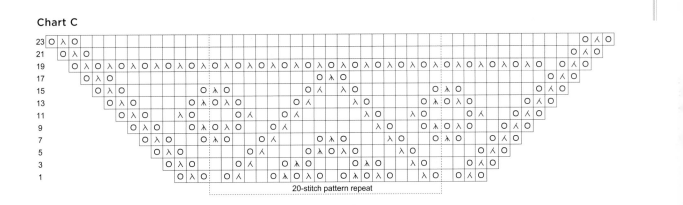

Chart B2

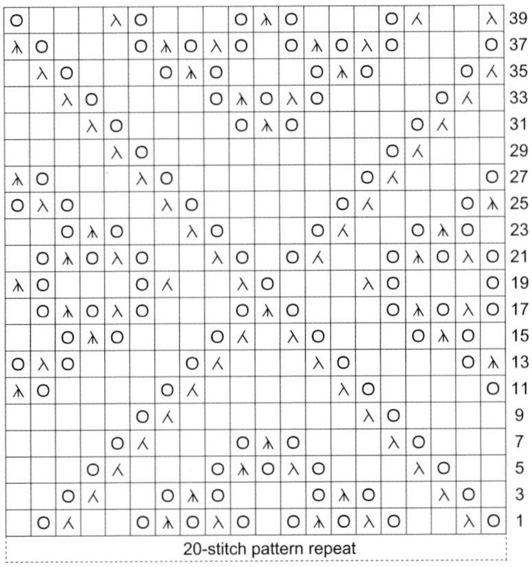

Chart B1

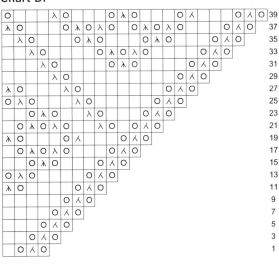

TIFFANY TRIANGLE SHAWL

A big fan of all things Art Deco and Art Nouveau, I designed this shawl's
geometric lace pattern with these styles in mind. And just like Tiffany-style
glasswork, this shawl perfectly balances structure and weightlessness.
I chose a slightly heavy lace-weight yarn to give the shawl a substantial presence—
and make it a good choice for knitters just getting started with lace.
Sized to fit as a wrap for petite women and a large scarf for taller women,
the Tiffany Triangle Shawl is a straightforward, fairly quick knit.

Skill Level
Intermediate

Size
One size

Finished Measurements
48" (122cm) across the top edge
and 21" (53.5cm) down the center
back unblocked, 66" (167.5cm)
across the top edge and 30"
(76cm) down the center back
blocked

Gauge
6 stitches = 1" (2.5cm) unblocked
in stockinette stitch

Needles
US size 5 (3.75mm), or size
needed to attain gauge

Yarn
1 skein Dream in Color Baby, 100%
superfine Australian superwash
merino, 4 oz (113g), 700 yd
(640m), November Muse
(1) Superfine

NOTE: Only odd-numbered (right-side) rows are shown in the charts.
All even-numbered (wrong-side) rows are worked as k3, p to the last 3
stitches, k3.

Shawl
Cast on 10 stitches.
Knit 4 rows even.

set up the lace pattern
Row 1: K3, yo, k1, yo, k2, yo, k1, yo, k3 (14 stitches
total).
Row 2: K3, purl to the last 3 stitches, k3.
Row 3: K3, yo, k3, yo, k2, yo, k3, yo, k3 (18 stitches
total).
Row 4: K3, p5 (place marker), p2 (place marker),
p5, k3.
The 2 stitches between the stitch markers are the 2
center stitches of the back of the Shawl.

chart a
K3, work across Chart A from right to left to the 1st
marker (slip marker), k2 (slip marker), work across
the same row of Chart A again from right to left,
k3. Continue to work Chart A. After completing all
44 rows of Chart A, you will have 106 total stitches
on your needles.
**NOTE: You will work each row of each chart twice—
once on either side of the 2 center stitches.**

b charts (pages 72–73)

K3, work across Chart B1 once, work across Chart B2 twice, work across Chart B3 once (slip marker), k2 (slip marker), work across Chart B1 once, work across Chart B2 twice, work across Chart B3 once, k3.

Continue to work the B charts as set. After completing all 44 rows of the 3 B charts, you will have 194 total stitches on your needles.

c charts (pages 72–73)

K3, work across Chart C1, work across Chart C2 4 times, work across Chart C3 (slip marker), k2 (slip marker), work across Chart C1, work across Chart C2 4 times, work across Chart C3, k3.

Continue to work the C charts as set. After completing all 46 rows of the C charts, you will have 286 total stitches on your needles.

chart d

K3, work across Chart D with 6 pattern repeats (slip marker), k2 (slip marker), work across Chart D with 6 pattern repeats, k3.

Continue to work Chart D. After completing all 12 rows of Chart D, you should have 310 total stitches on your needle.

Next row: K3, yo, k to 1st marker, yo (slip marker), k2 (slip marker), yo, k to last 3 stitches, yo, k3.

Next row: Knit across, removing markers as you come to them.

Bind off the remaining stitches loosely using the Russian Bind-Off. Weave in ends.

Finishing

Steam block or wet block your Shawl to the finished measurements. Keep the long top edge straight, and pull out the points of the edging on the 2 sides, pinning them in place with T-pins.

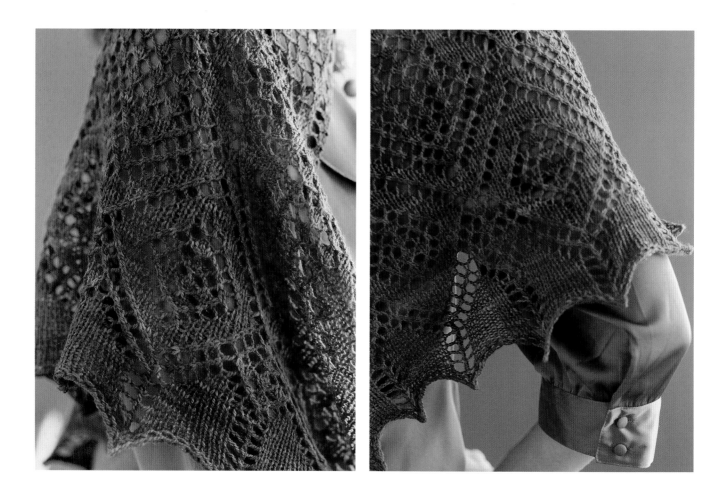

tiffany triangle shawl

Key

☐	K on RS, P on WS
O	YO
人	K2TOG
人	SSK
人	SL1 K2TOG PSSO

Chart A

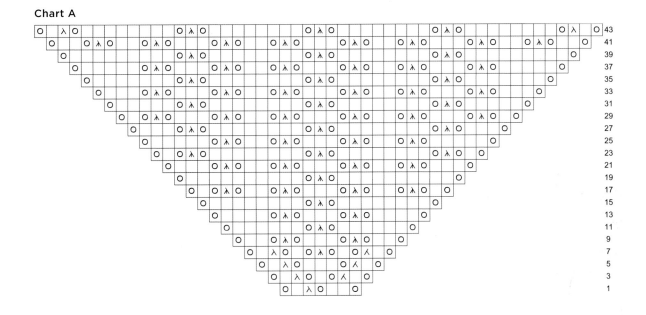

Chart D

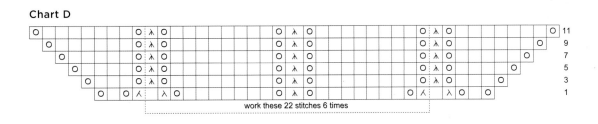

work these 22 stitches 6 times

tiffany triangle shawl

Chart B3

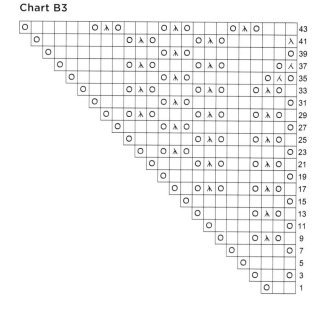

Chart B2

work these 22 stitches 2 times

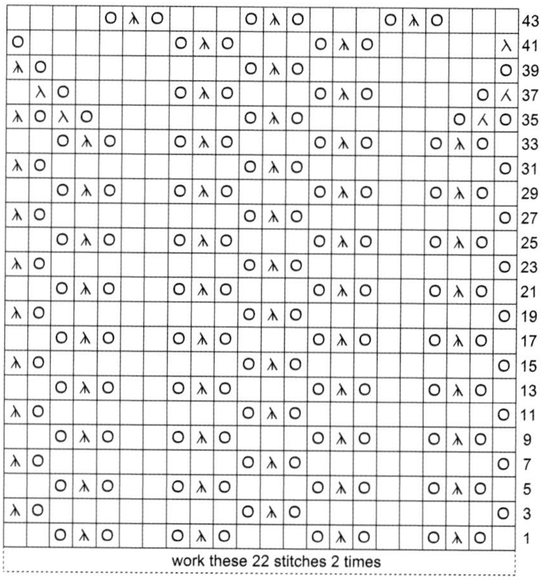

Chart C3

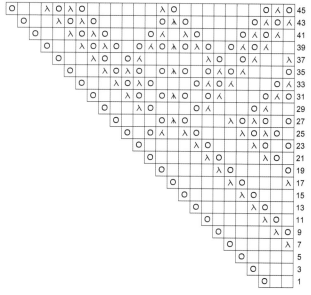

Chart C2

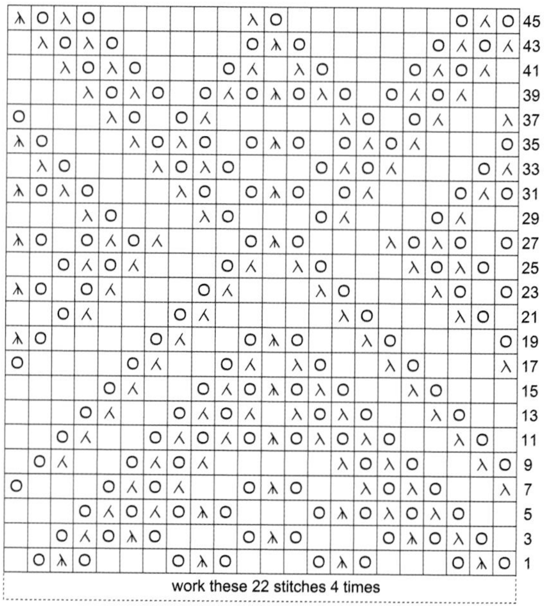

work these 22 stitches 4 times

Chart B1

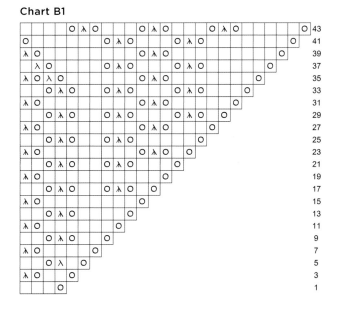

Chart C1

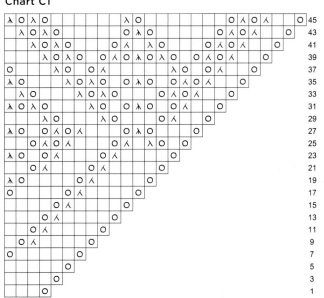

VORTEX SPIRAL SHAWL OR AFGHAN

This circular spiral shawl is a large undertaking, sizewise, but it is not difficult to knit. The body of the shawl is knit from the center out of simple lace stitches, and the only real challenge is working the knitted-on border. Knit this design in any yarn you desire. A lace- or fingering-weight yarn will yield a comfy shawl, a sport- or DK-weight yarn will make a snuggly baby blanket, and a worsted- or Aran-weight yarn will result in a cozy afghan. The yarn and needle requirements given for fingering- and worsted-weight yarns are only two possibilities.

Skill Level
Adventuresome Intermediate

Size
Two sizes: Shawl (Afghan)

Finished Measurements
SHAWL 48" (122cm) diameter unblocked, 60" (152.5cm) diameter blocked
AFGHAN 62" (157.5cm) diameter unblocked, 78" (198cm) diameter blocked

Gauge
SHAWL 5 stitches = 1" (2.5cm) unblocked in stockinette stitch
AFGHAN 4½ stitches = 1" (2.5cm) unblocked in stockinette stitch

Needles
SHAWL 1 set of 4 US size 6 (4mm) double-pointed needles, one 24" (60cm) circular needle, and one 32" (80cm) or 40" (100cm) circular needle (optional, see Notes), or size needed to attain gauge
AFGHAN 1 set of 4 US size 8 (5mm) double-pointed needles, one 24" (60cm) circular needle, and one 32" (80cm) or 40" (100cm) circular needle (optional, see Notes), or size needed to attain gauge

Yarn
SHAWL 4 skeins Dream in Color Smooshy, 100% superfine Australian superwash merino, 4 oz (113g), 450 yd (412m), Shiny Moss **(1)** Superfine
AFGHAN 10 skeins Cascade 220, 100% Peruvian Highland Wool, 3½ oz (100g), 220 yd (201m), Pumpkin Spice **(4)** Medium

NOTES: You will start your Shawl (Afghan) with the Circular Cast-On using 4 double-pointed needles. When you have enough stitches, transfer them to the 24" (60cm) (or longer) circular needle and mark the beginning of the round with a stitch marker.

The Shawl (Afghan) is worked from charts. Only the odd-numbered rounds are charted; on even-numbered rounds, knit around.

The Shawl (Afghan) is divided into 9 sections. I recommend that you place a stitch marker between each section. Each chart shows 1 section of the shawl, so on every round you will repeat the chart 9 times.

Shawl (Afghan)

Using the Circular Cast-On, cast on 9 stitches over 3 double-pointed needles (3 stitches per needle). Mark the beginning of the round and join, being careful not to twist your stitches.

chart a

Round 1: [Yo, k1, place marker] 9 times (18 stitches total).

NOTE: From this point forward, on every odd-numbered round through round 157, you will make a yarn over immediately after each marker. These increases are shown on the charts.

Round 2 (and all even-numbered rounds): Knit around. Work the rest of Chart A as shown. After completing all 38 rounds of Chart A, you will have 20 stitches in each of the 9 sections of your Shawl (Afghan) and a total of 180 stitches on your needles.

chart b

Work Chart B as shown. After completing through round 66 of Chart B, you will have 34 stitches in each of the 9 sections of your Shawl (Afghan) and a total of 306 stitches on your needles.

chart c

Work Chart C as shown. After completing through round 96 of Chart C, you will have 49 stitches in each of the 9 sections of your Shawl (Afghan) and a total of 441 stitches on your needles.

chart d

Work Chart D as shown. After completing through round 126 of Chart D, you will have 64 stitches in each of the 9 sections of your Shawl (Afghan) and a total of 576 stitches on your needles.

chart e

Work Chart E through round 157 as shown (see the instructions that follow for working round 158 with the Edging). After completing through round 157 of Chart E, you will have 80 stitches in each of the 9 sections of your Shawl (Afghan) and a total of 720 stitches on your needles.

edging

Round 158: Knit to 1 stitch before the end of the round, kfb (721 stitches total). Using the Knitted-On Cast-On and the working yarn, cast on 10 stitches. Turn the work.

K9, knit the 10th stitch together with 1 stitch from the edge of the Shawl (Afghan).

Begin working the Edging Chart: On odd-numbered rows, slip the 1st stitch purlwise with the yarn in front; on even-numbered rows, knit all stitches, knitting the last stitch of the chart together with 1 stitch on the edge of the Shawl (Afghan). (You will k6 edge stitches for every repeat of the edging pattern, for a total of 120 repeats of the edging pattern.)

After you have knit all the body stitches, bind off the edging loosely. Sew the edging cast-on edge to the edging cast-off edge. Weave in ends.

Finishing

Steam block or wet block your Shawl (Afghan) to the finished measurements. Pull out the points of the Edging, pinning them in place with T-pins.

vortex spiral shawl or afghan

Key

(blank)	K
O	YO
⋏	K2TOG
λ	SSK
⋏̣	SL1 K2TOG PSSO
U	K1TOG with 1 ST from body
V̲	SL1 as to P WYIF

Edging Chart

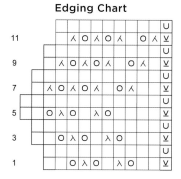

Chart B

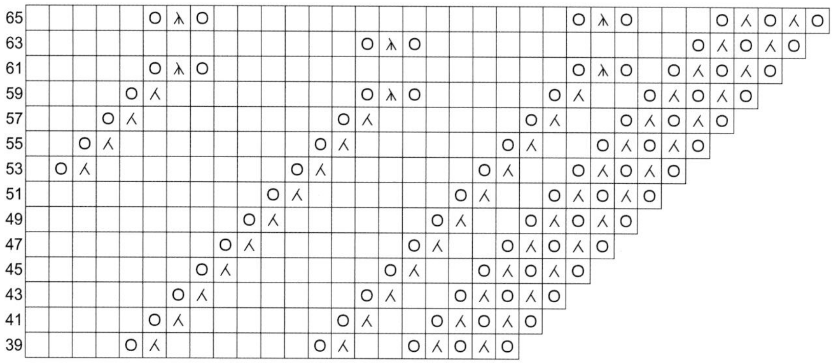

(chart, rows 39–65)

Chart A

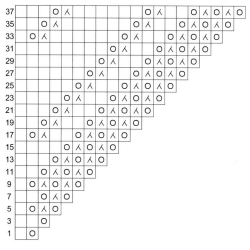

(chart, rows 1–37)

vortex spiral shawl or afghan

Chart E

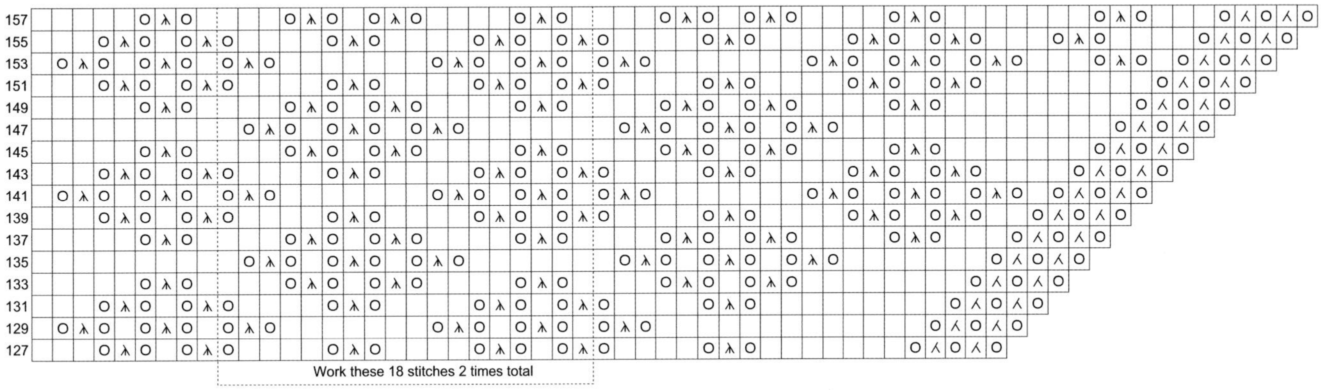
157
155
153
151
149
147
145
143
141
139
137
135
133
131
129
127
Work these 18 stitches 2 times total

Chart D

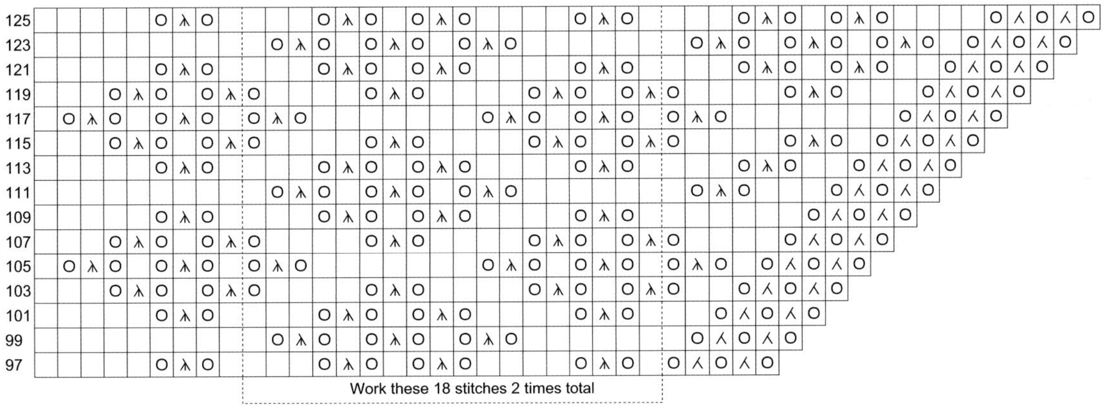
125
123
121
119
117
115
113
111
109
107
105
103
101
99
97
Work these 18 stitches 2 times total

Chart C

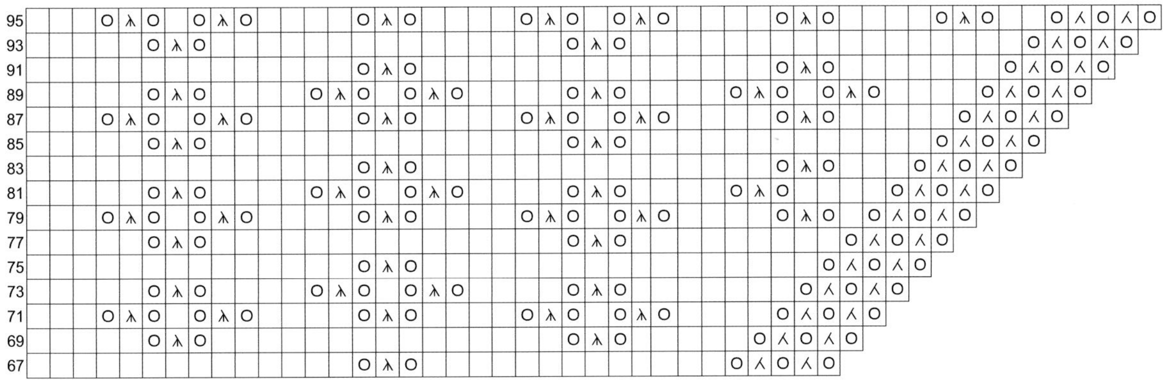
95
93
91
89
87
85
83
81
79
77
75
73
71
69
67

Vortex Spiral Shawl or Afghan 81

POOR POET'S MITTS

When I was young I thought it would be hugely romantic to be an impoverished artist living in an unheated garret with only my artistic genius to keep me warm. The older I get, the more practical I become, but I still have a bit of romance in my soul. While these mitts would be perfect for the artist living in my imagination, they also would be great for anyone who wants warm hands but needs to keep her fingers free. They are made from a fingering-weight sock yarn and are worked in an allover lace pattern. I chose a heathered solid yarn, but you can try a subtly variegated yarn for this design as well, because the lace pattern is strong enough to stand up to color changes.

Skill Level
Intermediate

Size
Women's Medium (Large)

Finished Measurements
6½ (7½)" (16.5 [19]cm) hand circumference

Gauge
8 stitches and 12 rows = 1" (2.5cm) unblocked in stockinette stitch

Needles
2 US size 1 (2.25mm) circular needles at least 16" (40cm) long (or 1 long circular needle and 1 set of 5 double-pointed needles), or size needed to attain gauge

Yarn
2 skeins Shibui Knits Sock, 100% superwash merino, 1¾ oz (50g), 191 yd (175m), Cranberry

1 Superfine

NOTE: The charts show odd-numbered rows only. On even-numbered rows, knit around.

Mitt (Make 2)
cuff
Cast on 52 (60) stitches, dividing them evenly between (or among) your needles: If you are using 2 circular needles, place 26 (30) stitches on each needle; if you are using double-pointed needles, place 13 (15) stitches on each of 4 needles. Join, being careful not to twist your stitches, and begin to work in the round. Work k2, p2 ribbing for 2" (5cm).

start the lace pattern
K1 (place marker), work the Lace Chart over the next 25 (29) stitches for the back of the hand (place marker), k26 (30).
Work the rest of the Lace Chart (8 rows total) once.

create the thumb gusset
Round 1: Work across the back of the hand in the pattern as set. For the right hand: K1 (place marker), k1, m1, k1, m1 (place marker), and knit to

For the left hand:
Knit to 3 stitches before the end of the round (place marker), k1, m1, k1, m1 (place marker), k1.

Round 2 (both hands): Continue in the pattern as set, working the Lace Chart across the back of the hand and knitting across the palm.

Round 3 (both hands): Work in pattern as set to the 1st marker (slip marker), k1, m1, knit to 2nd marker, m1 (slip marker), work in the pattern as set to the end of the round. (You will have 6 stitches between 2 gusset markers.)

Repeat rows 2 and 3 until you have 20 stitches total between the gusset markers.

Next round: Slip the 20 stitches between the gusset markers onto a length of waste yarn. Using a backward loop cast-on and the working yarn, cast on 2 stitches to bridge the gap created by removing the 20 thumb stitches (26 [30] stitches remain for the palm).

Work in the pattern as set for another 1³/₄" (4.5cm), or until the Mitt covers your hand up to the base of your fingers.

Work k2, p2 ribbing for 1" (2.5cm). Bind off in rib pattern.

thumb

Using double-pointed needles, pick up and knit the 20 stitches on the waste yarn, distributing them over 2 of the needles. Pick up and knit 4 stitches over the 2 stitches you cast on to continue the body of the Mitt.

Join, being careful not to twist your stitches, and knit 4 rounds.

Work 2 rounds of k1, p1 ribbing.

Bind off in rib pattern. Weave in ends.

Finishing

Wet block your Mitts to the finished measurements.

poor poet's mitts

Key

☐	K
O	YO
∧	K2TOG
λ	SSK
⋏	SL1 K2TOG PSSO

Medium Lace Chart

λ	O			O	λ	O			O	λ	O			O	λ	O			O	λ	O			O	λ	7
λ		O		O		λ		O		O		λ		O		O		λ		O		O		λ		5
		O	λ	O				O	λ	O				O	λ	O				O	λ	O				3
	O		λ		O		O		λ		O		O		λ		O		O		λ		O			1

| 25 | | 23 | | 21 | | 19 | | 17 | | 15 | | 13 | | 11 | | 9 | | 7 | | 5 | | 3 | | 1 | | |

Large Lace Chart

	O	λ	O				O	λ	O				O	λ	O				O	λ	O				O	λ	O		7
O		λ		O		O		λ		O		O		λ		O		O		λ		O		O		λ		O	5
			O	λ	O				O	λ	O				O	λ	O				O	λ	O						3
		O		λ		O		O		λ		O		O		λ		O		O		λ		O					1

| 29 | | 27 | | 25 | | 23 | | 21 | | 19 | | 17 | | 15 | | 13 | | 11 | | 9 | | 7 | | 5 | | 3 | | 1 |

ESPLANADE MITTENS

Lace was everywhere in the Victorian era, from doilies draped over every surface in an elegant parlor to dainty collars and shawls adorning fashionable ladies. I created this design—appropriate for any era—to fit the romantic notion of the fine ladies of that time strolling, arm in arm, along a chilly seaside esplanade. Knit from fingering-weight wool, these mittens feature a single lace motif repeated down the back of the hand and mirrored on each thumb. A solid or heathered yarn would work best; variegated colorways could obscure the lace pattern. These mittens are a good preliminary project for a beginning knitter who would like to eventually graduate to knitting gloves.

Skill Level
Adventuresome Beginner

Size
One size

Finished Measurements
8" (20.5cm) hand circumference

Gauge
7½ stitches and 9 rows = 1" (2.5cm) unblocked in stockinette stitch

Needles
1 set of 5 US size 2 (2.75mm) double-pointed needles, or size needed to attain gauge, and 1 set of 5 double-pointed needles 1 size smaller

Yarn
1 skein Dream in Color Smooshy Sock Yarn, 100% superfine Australian superwash merino, 4 oz (113g), 450 yd (412m), Grey Tabby
1 Superfine

Left Mitten
cuff
Using smaller needles, cast on 58 stitches over 4 double-pointed needles. Join, being careful not to twist your stitches, and begin to work in the round. Work in k1, p1 ribbing for 2" (5cm). Change to larger needles.
Allocate the stitches so that you have 30 stitches for the back of the hand on 2 double-pointed needles and 28 stitches for the palm on 2 double-pointed needles. (Alternatively, you can place each set of stitches onto 2 circular needles.)
Knit 2 rounds.

start lace pattern and left gusset
NOTE: The Left Gusset Chart shows all rounds, but the Lace Chart shows only odd-numbered rounds; on even-numbered rounds, knit around.
Back of hand: K9 (place marker), work the Lace Chart over the next 13 stitches (place marker), k8.
Palm: Work the Left Gusset Chart.
Continue to work the Lace Chart on the back of the hand and the Left Gusset Chart on the palm. When you reach the increase row on the Left Gusset Chart, increase 2 stitches for the thumb gusset where shown on the chart. Work each increase by picking up the strand between 2 stitches and knitting it, twisting it as you knit.

Work until you have completed all 21 rows of the Left Gusset Chart.

Next round: Work across the back of the hand in the lace pattern as set, k22, slip the next 17 stitches to a stitch holder or a length of waste yarn, cast on 5 stitches, k3 (30 palm stitches and 60 stitches total).

Continue working until you have completed all 47 rows of the Lace Chart.

Next round: Knit all stitches.

Repeat this round until the Mitten is ½" (13mm) shy of the desired total length.

esplanade mittens

Key

	K
O	YO
⋏	K2TOG
λ	SSK
λ	SL1 K2TOG PSSO
ŏ	INC 1

Lace Chart

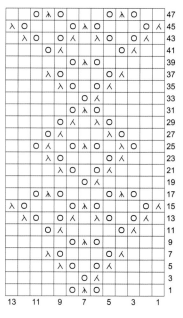

Left Gusset Chart

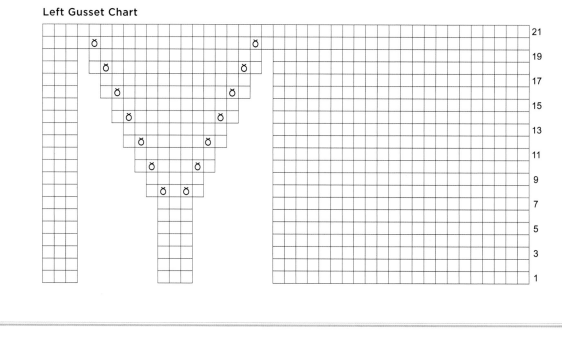

Decrease for the top of the hand: **Round 1:** K2, ssk, k23, k2tog, k3, ssk, k23, k2tog, k1 (4 stitches decreased).

Round 2: K2, ssk, k21, k2tog, k3, ssk, k21, k2tog, k1 (4 stitches decreased).

Continue in this manner, working 2 fewer stitches between decreases on each round until you complete 7 decrease rounds. (You will have 32 stitches on the needles: 16 stitches each for the back of the hand and the palm.)

Divide the remaining stitches over 2 needles and graft them together, or do a 3-needle bind-off to close the top of the mitten.

Right Gusset Chart

Thumb Chart

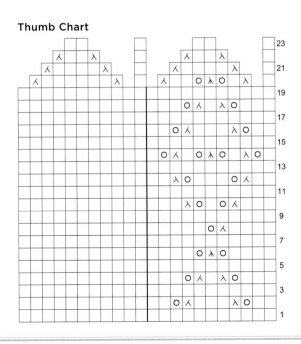

Work the 1st decrease at the top of the thumb as follows: K1, ssk, work in pattern to the next decrease, k2tog, k1, ssk, knit across to the next decrease, k2tog.

Continue in this manner until you have completed the Thumb Chart (6 stitches remain).

Break the working yarn, thread it through a tapestry needle, weave the yarn through the live stitches twice, pull firmly to tighten, and fasten off. Weave in ends.

Right Mitten

Work the Cuff as for the Left Mitten.

Change to the larger needles, and divide the stitches as for the Left Mitten.

Knit 2 rounds.

start lace pattern and right gusset

NOTE: The Right Gusset Chart shows all rows, but the Lace Chart shows only odd-numbered rounds; on even-numbered rounds, knit around.

Palm: Work the Right Gusset Chart as for the Left Mitten (Left Gusset Chart).

Back of hand: K8, work the Lace Chart over the next 13 stitches, k9.

Continue to work the Right Gusset Chart on the palm and the Lace Chart on the back of the hand (21 rows total).

Next row: K3, slip 17 stitches to a stitch holder, cast on 5 stitches, k22, work across the back of the hand in pattern as set (30 palm stitches and 60 stitches total).

Complete the rest of the Right Mitten as for the Left Mitten.

Finishing

Wet block your Mittens to the finished measurements.

thumb

Slip the first 3 thumb gusset stitches from the stitch holder onto 1 double-pointed needle, the next 11 stitches onto another double-pointed needle, and the remaining 3 stitches from the holder onto a 3rd double-pointed needle.

Pick up and knit 5 stitches over the cast-on edge on the 1st round (22 stitches total).

Join, being careful not to twist your stitches, and begin to work in the round. Work the Thumb Chart, starting with the needle holding 11 stitches.

MITTEN MAGIC

Feeling adventuresome? Use the Esplanade Mitten pattern as a template to create your own mitten design.

You can easily substitute a different lace motif for the one I have created for this pattern. My lace chart is 13 stitches wide by 47 rows high, but you don't have to choose a motif exactly that size. The back of the hand is 30 stitches wide. I suggest that you leave 3 or 4 plain stockinette stitches on each side of the lace for stability, so you could use a chart up to 22 or 24 stitches wide. You also have a bit of leeway in the number of rows in your chart, going up or down a few rows. You could even center a smaller pattern on the back of your mitten—it's up to you!

The same goes for the thumb pattern: leave it plain or keep it fancy by replacing my thumb chart with a smaller version of the motif you design for the main lace pattern.

BOBBLE GLOVES

Have you knit more mittens (or fingerless mitts) than you care to admit?
Are you ready to try something a little more challenging? Knit some gloves! I think
gloves are more interesting to knit than mittens because knitting the fingers is fast
and fun. Use double-pointed needles, 5" (12.5cm) or shorter, to whip up all ten fingers
in a flash. These gloves feature a delicate border of lace and bobbles, which makes
them a great accessory to complete a steampunk or goth look while still appealing to
those with a more mainstream fashion sense. What's more, bobbles are really quite
easy to make, so don't let lack of experience keep you from trying this pattern.

Skill Level
Adventuresome Intermediate

Size
Women's Small (Medium)

Finished Measurements
6½ (8)" (16.5 [20.5]cm) hand circumference

Gauge
7½ stitches and 11 rows = 1" (2.5cm) unblocked in stockinette stitch

Needles
1 set of 5 US size 1 (2.25mm) double-pointed needles, or size needed to attain gauge, and 1 set of 5 US size 3 (3.25mm) double-pointed needles

Yarn
1 (2) skeins Alchemy Juniper Elements, 100% superwash merino, 1¾ oz (50g), 232 yd (212m), Amethyst **1** Superfine

NOTES: The measurements given for knitting the length of each finger are approximate for an average hand. If you are knitting gloves for someone with fingers shorter or longer than average, simply knit fewer or more rounds to achieve the desired lengths. Just be sure to make a note of how long you knit each finger on the 1st glove so you can easily knit the 2nd glove to match.

If you find holes at the bases of the thumb and/or fingers where you have cast-on or picked up stitches, no worries—carefully sew them up with a bit of leftover project yarn when you're weaving in your ends. (Alternatively, for the thumb and fingers, pick up or cast on more stitches than directed to in the pattern, then on the 1st round of knitting, decrease back down to the total number of stitches indicated in the pattern.)

If bobbles are new to you, see Knit in the Know: Bobbles (page 94).

KNIT IN THE KNOW: BOBBLES

Regardless of whether you've ever worked a bobble before, the following instructions will help you to make a perfect bobble in no time.

TO MAKE 1 BOBBLE [K1, p1, k1, p1] in 1 stitch. Turn. K4. Turn. K4. Turn. K4. Turn. Lift, 1 at a time (in order), the 2nd, 3rd, and 4th stitches over the 1st stitch and then k that stitch.

Glove (Make 2)

border

Cast on 50 (60) stitches onto 4 of the larger double-pointed needles. Join, being careful not to twist your stitches, and begin to work in the round. Work the Border Lace Chart 5 (6) times.

Continue to work the Border Lace Chart until all 10 rounds of the chart have been completed.

For size Small only: As you work round 10, the last round of the chart, increase 2 stitches evenly (52 stitches total).

ribbing

Change to the smaller size needles and work in k1, p1 ribbing for 1" (2.5cm).

Next round: Knit to 1 stitch before the end of the round, increase 1 stitch by picking up the strand between 2 stitches and knitting it, twisting it as you knit (53 [61] stitches total).

create the thumb gusset

K26 (30) (place marker), m1, k1, m1 (place marker), knit to the end of the round (2 stitches increased, and 3 stitches between the gusset markers).

Knit 1 round even.

Increase round: Knit to the marker (slip marker), m1, knit to next marker, m1 (slip marker), knit to the end of the round.

Knit 2 rounds even.

Knit 1 increase round.

Continue to knit, working increase rounds every 3rd round 5 (6) times more (17 [19] stitches total between gusset markers).

Knit 3 rounds even.

Next round: Slip the 17 (19) stitches between the gusset markers onto a stitch holder or a length of waste yarn and remove the markers. Using a backward loop cast-on, cast on 1 stitch with the working yarn to close the gap, knit to the end of the round (53 [61] stitches total on the needles). Work even until the hand above the ribbing measures 3 (3½)" (7.5 [9]cm) or reaches the base of the little finger.

little finger

On the next round, k6 (8) stitches, place the next 42 (46) stitches on a length of waste yarn, cast on 1 stitch with a backward loop cast-on, rejoin to the remainder of the stitches on the needle, knit to the end of the round (12 [16] stitches total).

Arrange these stitches over 3 double-pointed needles, and knit in the round until the finger measures 1¾ (2)" (4.5 [5]cm).

Decrease for the top of the finger: Next round: K2tog around (6 [8] stitches remain).

Next round: K2tog around (3 [4] stitches remain). Break the working yarn, thread its tail through a tapestry needle, weave the yarn through the remaining stitches twice, pull firmly to tighten, and fasten off on the wrong side.

continue knitting the hand

Slip the stitches from the waste yarn back onto the needles. To close the gap created by the little finger, pick up and knit 2 stitches at the base of the finger (44 [48] stitches total).

Knit 3 rounds even.

ring finger

Place the first and last 8 stitches on double-pointed needles and slip the remainder of the stitches to waste yarn. Using a backward loop cast-on, cast on 1 (2) stitch(es) to close the gap (17 [18] stitches total).

Arrange these stitches over 3 double-pointed needles, and knit in the round until the finger measures $2^3/_4$ (3)" (7 [7.5] cm).

Decrease for the top of the finger: K2tog around (8 [9] stitches remain).

NOTE: For size Small, end with a k3tog on the last 3 stitches.

K2tog around (4 stitches remain).

NOTE: For size Medium, end with a k3tog on the last 3 stitches.

Break the working yarn, thread its tail through a tapestry needle, weave the yarn through the remaining stitches twice, pull firmly to tighten, and fasten off on the wrong side.

middle finger

Slip the first and last 7 (8) stitches from the waste yarn onto double-pointed needles. Pick up and knit 2 stitches along the cast-on edge of the ring finger, and cast on 1 (2) stitch(es) with a backward loop cast-on to close the gap (17 [20] stitches total).

Arrange these stitches over 3 double-pointed needles, and knit in the round until the finger measures 3 ($3^1/_4$)" (7.5 [8]cm).

Decrease for the top of the finger: K2tog around (8 [10] stitches remain).

NOTE: For size Small, end with a k3tog on the last 3 stitches.

K2tog around (4 [5] stitches remain).

Break the working yarn, thread its tail through a tapestry needle, weave the yarn through the remaining stitches twice, pull firmly to tighten, and fasten off on the wrong side.

index finger

Slip the remaining 14 (16) stitches from the waste yarn onto double-pointed needles. Pick up and knit 1 (2) stitch(es) to close the gap (15 [18] stitches total).

Arrange these stitches over 3 double-pointed needles, and knit in the round until the finger measures $2^3/_4$ (3)" (7 [7.5] cm).

Decrease for the top of the finger: K2tog around (7 [9] stitches remain).

NOTE: For size Small, end with a k3tog on the last 3 stitches.

K2tog around to the last stitch, k1 (4 [5] stitches remain).

Break the working yarn, thread its tail through a tapestry needle, weave the yarn through the remaining stitches twice, pull firmly to tighten, and fasten off on the wrong side.

thumb

Place the 17 (19) gusset stitches from the waste yarn on double-pointed needles. Pick up and knit 1 stitch along the cast-on edge between the thumb and the hand so that you have a total of 18 (20) stitches on your needles for the thumb.
Arrange these stitches over 3 double-pointed needles, and work in the round until the thumb measures 1³/₄ (2)" (4.5 [5] cm).

Decrease for the top of the thumb: K2tog around, so that 9 (10) stitches remain.
K2tog around (for smaller size end with a k3tog on the last 3 stitches), so that 4 (5) stitches remain.
Break the working yarn, thread its tail through a tapestry needle, weave the yarn through the remaining stitches twice, pull firmly to tighten, fasten off on the wrong side. Weave in ends.

Finishing

Wet block your Gloves to the finished measurements, being careful to pull the bobbles out neatly from the bottom of the border. If you have glove forms in the correct size, slip dampened gloves over the forms until completely dry.

bobble gloves

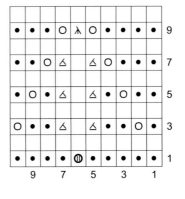

Key

	K on RS, P on WS
•	P on RS, K on WS
O	YO
λ	SL1 K2TOG PSSO
⋏	P2TOG
⑩	Make bobble (see instructions in glove pattern)

Border Lace Chart

DELICATE VINES
SOCKS

DELICATE VINES SOCKS

If you know me, you know I love to design and knit socks. In my previous books, I included all kinds of sock designs, but my favorites are lace. If you are new to sock knitting, I recommend that you start with the Delicate Vines Socks. The lace pattern is simple and easy to remember, and the heavy sportweight yarn makes them a speedy knit. The heel is an easy one: After working gusset increases, do a series of short rows with decreases (but no wrapping of stitches). The resulting socks are soft and cushy—equally great for padding around the house and wearing in boots.

Skill Level
Adventuresome Beginner

Size
Women's Extra Small (Small, Medium, Large, Extra Large)

Finished Measurements
6³/₄ (7¹/₄, 8, 8¹/₂, 9¹/₄)" (17 [18.5, 20.5, 21.5, 23.5]cm) foot circumference, 7¹/₂" (19cm) high (from the bottom of the foot to the top of the cuff)

Gauge
6¹/₂ stitches and 9 rows = 1" (2.5cm) unblocked in stockinette stitch

Needles
2 US size 2 (2.75mm) circular needles at least 16" (40cm) long, or size needed to attain gauge (see Notes)

Yarn
1 skein Fiesta Boomerang, 100% Extra Fine superwash merino, 5 oz (142g), 320 yd (293m), White Zinfandel **2** Fine

NOTES: Knit these socks using your favorite method: a set of double-pointed needles, 2 short circular needles, or 1 long circular needle (the Magic Loop method). The pattern instructions divide the stitches into 2 groups: the instep (top of the foot, needle 1) and the sole (bottom of the foot, needle 2). For complete instructions on my favorite method of sock knitting, including cast-ons, refer to my previous books, *Socks from the Toe Up* and *Toe-Up Socks for Every Body*.

When you work the "make 1" (m1) increases for the toe and the gusset, do a lifted increase or knit into the front and back of the stitch (kfb), whichever you prefer. I prefer the latter method, which tends to make a neater increase with no hole.

The charts show odd-numbered rows only. On even-numbered rows, knit around.

Sock (Make 2)

toe

Using a toe-up cast-on method, (see Notes), cast on a total of 20 (20, 24, 28, 28) stitches—10 (10, 12, 14, 14) on each needle. Knit across the stitches on each needle once.

Next round: Needle 1: K1, m1, knit across to the last stitch, m1, k1 (2 stitches increased). Needle 2: K1, m1, knit across to the last stitch, m1, k1 (2 stitches increased).

Round 2: Knit around even.

Repeat these 2 rounds until you have a total of 44 (48, 52, 56, 60) stitches—22 (24, 26, 28, 30) stitches on each needle.

start the lace pattern

Needle 1: Work across row 1 of the Lace Chart for the appropriate size.

Needle 2: Knit across.

Continue in this manner, working all 4 rows of the Lace Chart until the sock measures approximately 2–2¹⁄₂" (5–6.5cm) less than the total desired length of the foot.

create the gusset

Round 1: Needle 1: Work in the lace pattern as set. Needle 2: K1, m1, knit across to the last stitch, m1, k1.

Round 2: Needle 1: Work in the lace pattern as set. Needle 2: Knit all stitches.

Repeat rounds 1 and 2 until you have 36 (40, 44, 48, 52) stitches total on needle 2.

Work across needle 1 in pattern.

---

delicate vines socks

Key

☐	K
O	YO
⋏	K2TOG

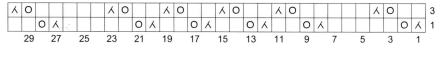

Extra Small Lace Chart

Row 3 (top) and Row 1 (bottom); columns labeled 21, 19, 17, 15, 13, 11, 9, 7, 5, 3, 1.

Small Lace Chart

Row 3 (top) and Row 1 (bottom); columns labeled 23, 21, 19, 17, 15, 13, 11, 9, 7, 5, 3, 1.

Medium Lace Chart

Row 3 (top) and Row 1 (bottom); columns labeled 25, 23, 21, 19, 17, 15, 13, 11, 9, 7, 5, 3, 1.

Large Lace Chart

Row 3 (top) and Row 1 (bottom); columns labeled 27, 25, 23, 21, 19, 17, 15, 13, 11, 9, 7, 5, 3, 1.

Extra Large Lace Chart

Row 3 (top) and Row 1 (bottom); columns labeled 29, 27, 25, 23, 21, 19, 17, 15, 13, 11, 9, 7, 5, 3, 1.

turn the heel

Working back and forth on the 36 (40, 44, 48, 52) sole stitches on needle 2 only:

Row 1: K21 (23, 25, 27, 29), ssk, k1, turn.

Row 2: Sl1, p7, p2tog, p1, turn.

Row 3: Sl1, k8, ssk, k1, turn.

Row 4: Sl1, p9, p2tog, p1, turn.

Row 5: Sl1, k10, ssk, k1, turn.

Row 6: Sl1, p11, p2tog, p1, turn.

Continue in this manner, working 1 more stitch before the decrease on each subsequent round until all the stitches are worked and you have 22 (24, 26, 28, 30) stitches on the needle. Turn needle 2.

Next row: Knit across even.

leg

Work across needle 1 in the lace pattern as set. Work the same row of the Lace Chart across needle 2.

Continue to work the Lace Chart on both needles until the leg measures approximately 6" (15cm) above the heel or approximately 1½" (3.8cm) less than your desired total length, ending after working row 2 or row 4 of the Lace Chart. Work in k1, p1 ribbing for 1½" (3.8cm). Bind off loosely in rib pattern. Weave in ends.

Finishing

If desired, wet block your Socks to the finished measurements. If you own sock blockers, slip dampened socks over the sock blockers until completely dry.

NOTE: I do not always block socks because they stretch out nicely while being worn; whether to block is up to you.

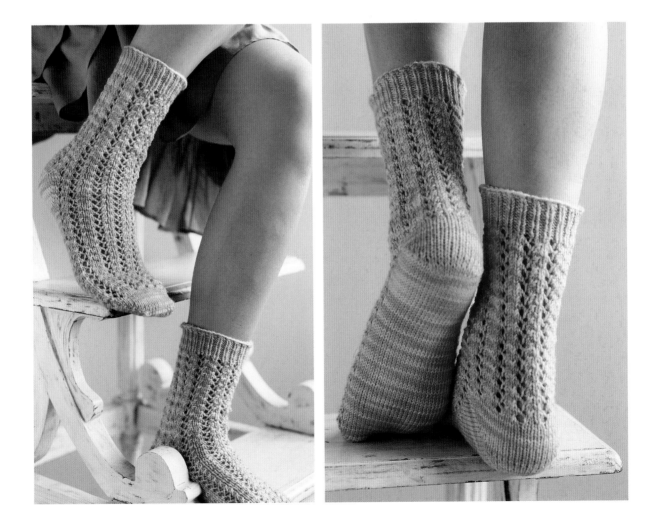

DIAMOND LACE SOCKS

One of the beauties of lace socks is their inherent stretchiness. The more lace on the sock, the more elastic it becomes, and the better it will fit a wide range of foot and leg sizes. This pattern features a large lace design that is worked in a fingering-weight yarn over the entire width of the sock, so the resulting socks are very stretchy. The design is suitable for a solid color or a colorway with subtle shading; it is best to stay away from wildly variegated yarns for these socks as the variegation will fight with and obscure the lace pattern.

Skill Level
Intermediate

Size
Women's Extra Small (Small, Medium, Large, Extra Large)

Finished Measurements
6 (7, 8, 9, 10)" (15 [18, 20.5, 23, 25.5]cm) foot circumference, 7½" (19cm) high (from the bottom of the foot to the top of the cuff)

Gauge
8 stitches and 12 rows = 1" (2.5cm) unblocked in stockinette stitch

Needles
2 US size 1 (2.25mm) circular needles at least 16" (40cm) long, or size needed to attain gauge (see Notes)

Yarn
2 skeins Shibui Knits Sock, 100% superwash merino, 1¾ oz (50g), 191 yd (175m), Periwinkle
1 Superfine

NOTES: Knit these socks using your favorite sock-knitting method: a set of double-pointed needles, 2 short circular needles, or 1 long circular needle (for the Magic Loop method). The pattern divides the stitches into 2 groups: the instep (top of the foot, needle 1) and the sole (bottom of the foot, needle 2). For complete instructions on my favorite method of sock knitting, including cast-ons, refer to my previous books, *Socks from the Toe Up* and *Toe-Up Socks for Every Body.*

When you work the "make 1" (m1) increases for the toe and the gusset, do a lifted increase or knit into the front and back of the stitch (kfb), whichever you prefer. I prefer the latter method, which tends to make a neater increase with no hole.

The charts show odd-numbered rows only. On even-numbered rows, knit around.

Sock (Make 2)

toe

Using a toe-up cast-on method (see Notes), cast on a total of 22 (26, 30, 34, 38) stitches—11 (13, 15, 17, 19) on each needle. Knit across the stitches on each needle once.

Round 1: Needle 1: Kfb, knit until 2 stitches remain, kfb, k1 (2 stitches increased). Needle 2: Kfb, knit until 2 stitches remain, kfb, k1 (2 stitches increased).

Round 2: Knit around even.

Repeat these 2 rounds until you have a total of 50 (58, 66, 74, 82) stitches—25 (29, 33, 37, 41) on each needle.

diamond lace socks

Key

☐	K
O	YO
⋏	K2TOG
λ	SSK

Extra Small Lace Chart

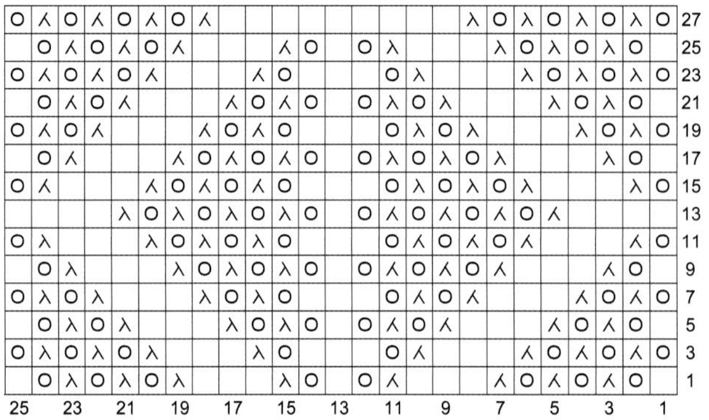

(chart, columns numbered 25, 23, 21, 19, 17, 15, 13, 11, 9, 7, 5, 3, 1; rows numbered 27, 25, 23, 21, 19, 17, 15, 13, 11, 9, 7, 5, 3, 1)

Small Lace Chart

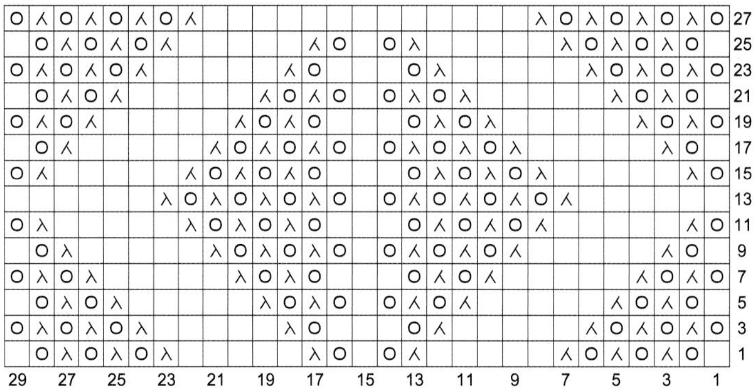

(chart, columns numbered 29, 27, 25, 23, 21, 19, 17, 15, 13, 11, 9, 7, 5, 3, 1; rows numbered 27, 25, 23, 21, 19, 17, 15, 13, 11, 9, 7, 5, 3, 1)

Medium Lace Chart

(chart, columns numbered 33, 31, 29, 27, 25, 23, 21, 19, 17, 15, 13, 11, 9, 7, 5, 3, 1; rows numbered 27, 25, 23, 21, 19, 17, 15, 13, 11, 9, 7, 5, 3, 1)

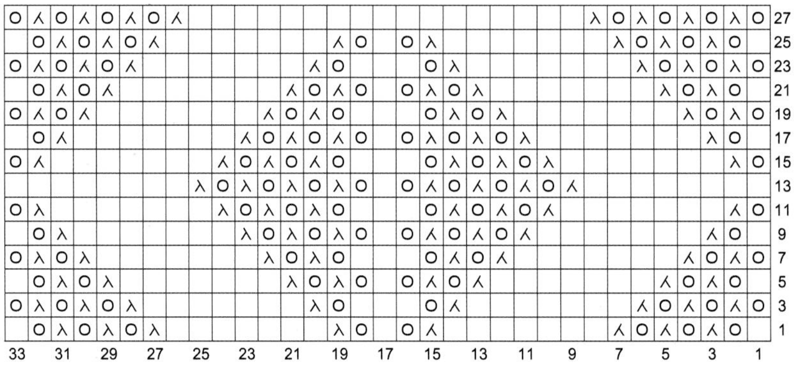

start the lace pattern

Needle 1: Work across row 1 of the Lace Chart.

Needle 2: Knit across.

Continue in this manner, working as many repeats of the Lace Chart pattern as needed until the sock measures approximately 3" (7.5cm) less than the total length of the foot.

create the gusset

Round 1: Needle 1: Work in the lace pattern as set.

Needle 2: Kfb, knit across until 2 stitches remain, kfb, k1.

Round 2: Needle 1: Work in the lace pattern as set.

Needle 2: Knit all stitches.

Repeat rounds 1 and 2 until you have 43 (49, 55, 61, 67) total sole stitches on needle 2.

Next Row: Needle 1: Work in lace pattern as set.

turn the heel

You will now work back and forth on the stitches on needle 2 and will not knit the stitches on needle 1 while turning the heel. Turn heel as follows:

Row 1 (RS): K29 (33, 37, 41, 45), kfb, k1, w&t.

Row 2 (WS): P18 (20, 22, 24, 26), pfb, p1, w&t.

Row 3: K16 (18, 20, 22, 24), kfb, k1, w&t.

Row 4: P14 (16, 18, 20, 22), pfb, p1, w&t.

Row 5: K12 (14, 16, 18, 20), kfb, k1, w&t.

Row 6: P10 (12, 14, 16, 18), pfb, p1, w&t.

Row 7: K8 (10, 12, 14, 16), kfb, k1, w&t.

Row 8: P6 (8, 10, 12, 14), pfb, p1, w&t.

Needle 2 now holds 51 (57, 63, 69, 75) stitches, having just completed a wrong-side row. On the right side, knit to the end of needle 2. Work across the instep stitches on needle 1 in the chart pattern.

Large Lace Chart

Extra Large Lace Chart

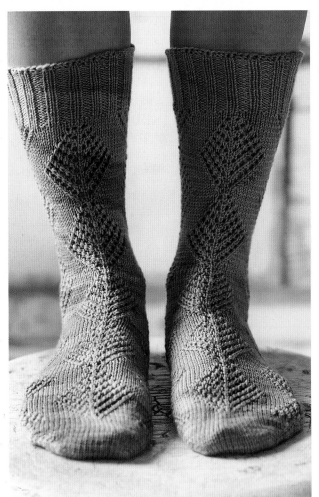

heel flap

Working back and forth on the heel stitches on needle 2 only:

Row 1 (RS): K37 (42, 47, 52, 57), ssk, turn.

Row 2: Sl1 as if to knit, p23 (27, 31, 35, 39), p2tog, turn.

Row 3: [Sl1 as if to knit, k1] 12 (14, 16, 18, 20) times, ssk, turn.

Repeat rows 2 and 3 until all side stitches have been worked; end having worked row 2 (25 [29, 33, 37, 41] stitches on needle 2). Turn your work.

Next row: Knit across, increasing 2 stitches evenly above the heel (27 [31, 35, 39, 43] stitches on needle 2).

leg

Begin working in the round again, making sure to work the same row of the Lace Chart over needle 2 as worked on needle 1:

Needle 1: Work the Lace Chart pattern as set.

Needle 2: K1, work the appropriate row of the Lace Chart, k1 (27 [31, 35, 39, 43] stitches on needle 2). Continue to work the pattern as set on both needles until the leg measures approximately 6" (15cm) above the heel or approximately 1½" (3.8cm) less than your desired total length, ending after row 28 of the Lace Chart.

Work in k1, p1 ribbing for 1½" (3.8cm).

Bind off loosely in rib pattern. Weave in ends.

Finishing

If desired, wet block your Socks to the finished measurements. If you own sock blockers, slip dampened socks over the sock blockers until completely dry.

NOTE: I do not always block socks because they stretch out nicely while being worn; whether to block is up to you.

VINTAGE KNEESOCKS

VINTAGE KNEESOCKS

Sock knitters who keep an eye on the fashion runway know that kneesocks have made a big comeback since the days when these socks were de rigueur only for teenaged girls in prep school. Today, kneesocks are peeking out from boots and booties and they are even being paired with dainty ballet flats. The dense lace pattern of this design makes a nicely stretchy sock, and stretchy is a feature you want for a great fit. What's more, calf increases are worked on the back of the leg to further ensure a fit that won't quit.

Skill Level
Advanced

Size
Women's Small (Medium, Large, Extra Large)

Finished Measurements
6½ (7½, 8½, 9½)" (16.5 [19, 21.5, 24]cm) foot circumference, 18" (45.5cm) high (from the bottom of the foot to the top of the cuff)

Gauge
8 stitches and 12 rows = 1" (2.5cm) unblocked in stockinette stitch

Needles
2 US size 1 (2.25mm) circular needles at least 16" (40cm) long, or size needed to attain gauge (see Notes)

Yarn
1 (1, 2, 2) skeins Dream in Color Smooshy Sock Yarn, 100% superfine Australian superwash merino, 4 oz (113g), 450 yd (412m), Crying Dove 🔲1 Superfine

NOTES: For the Small and Medium sizes, knit to fit a foot that is approximately a US shoe size 9 or smaller, you will be able to make 1 pair of kneesocks from 1 skein of the specified yarn. You may need 2 skeins for larger shoe sizes or if you increase the leg length of the socks.

Knit these socks using your favorite sock-knitting method: a set of double-pointed needles, 2 short circular needles, or 1 long circular (the Magic Loop method). The pattern divides the stitches into 2 groups: the instep (top of the foot, needle 1) and the sole (bottom of the foot, needle 2). For complete instructions on my favorite method of sock knitting, including cast-ons, refer to my previous books, *Socks from the Toe Up* and *Toe-Up Socks for Every Body*.

When you work the "make 1" (m1) increases for the toe and the gusset, do a lifted increase or knit into the front and back of the stitch (kfb), whichever you prefer. I prefer the latter method, which tends to make a neater increase with no hole.

The charts show odd-numbered rows only. On even-numbered rows, knit around.

Sock (Make 2)

toe

Using a toe-up cast-on method (see Notes), cast on a total of 22 (26, 30, 34) stitches—11 (13, 15, 17) on each needle. Knit across the stitches on each needle once.

Round 1: Needle 1: K1, m1, knit until the last stitch, m1, k1 (2 stitches increased). Needle 2: K1, m1, knit until the last stitch, m1, k1 (2 stitches increased).

Round 2: Knit around even.

Repeat these 2 rounds until you have a total of 50 (58, 66, 74) stitches—25 (29, 33, 37) stitches on each needle.

start the lace pattern

Needle 1: Work the 1st row of the Lace Chart.

Needle 2: Knit across even.

Continue in this manner, working the 30-row Lace Chart as many times as necessary until the sock measures approximately 3" (7.5cm) shy of the total length of the foot.

create the gusset

Round 1: Needle 1: Work in the lace pattern as set. Needle 2: K1, m1, knit to the last stitch, m1, k1.

Round 2: Needle 1: Work in the lace pattern as set. Needle 2: Knit all stitches.

Repeat rounds 1 and 2 until you have 43 (49, 55, 61) stitches on needle 2.

Next row: Needle 1: Work in lace pattern as set.

turn the heel

Working back and forth on the 43 (49, 55, 61) sole stitches on needle 2 only:

Row 1 (RS): K29 (33, 37, 41), kfb, k1, w&t.

Row 2 (WS): P18 (20, 22, 24), pfb, p1, w&t.

Row 3: K16 (18, 20, 22), kfb, k1, w&t.

Row 4: P14 (16, 18, 20), pfb, p1, w&t.

Row 5: K12 (14, 16, 18), kfb, k1, w&t.

Row 6: P10 (12, 14, 16), pfb, p1, w&t.

Row 7: K8 (10, 12, 14), kfb, k1, w&t.

Row 8: P6 (8, 10, 12), pfb, p1, w&t (51 [57, 63, 69] stitches on needle 2).

Turn needle 2 to the right side again and work 1 round: Needle 2: Knit across even. Needle 1: Work in the lace pattern as set.

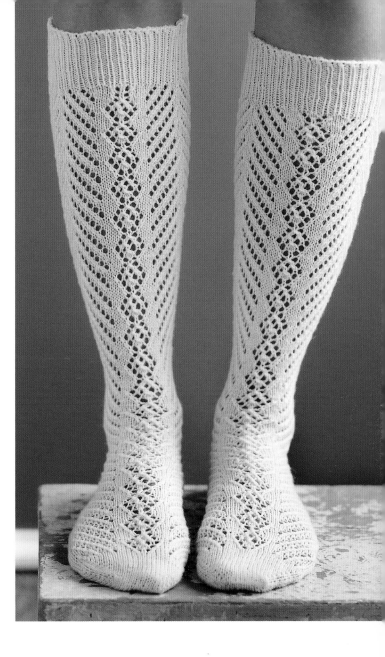

heel flap

Working back and forth on the heel stitches on needle 2 only:

Row 1 (RS): K37 (42, 47, 52), ssk, turn.

Row 2 (WS): Sl1 as if to knit, p23 (27, 31, 35), p2tog, turn.

Row 3: [Sl1, k1] 12 (14, 16, 18) times, ssk, turn.

Repeat rows 2 and 3 until all side stitches have been worked, ending after row 2. Turn.

Next row: Knit across (25 [29, 33, 37] stitches on needle 2).

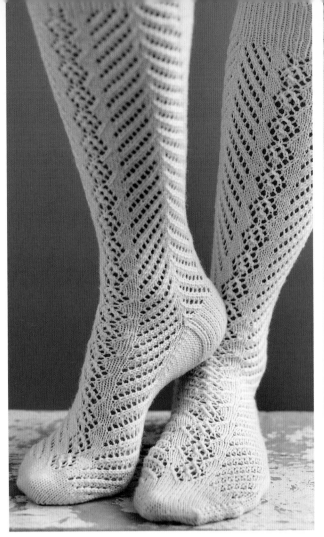
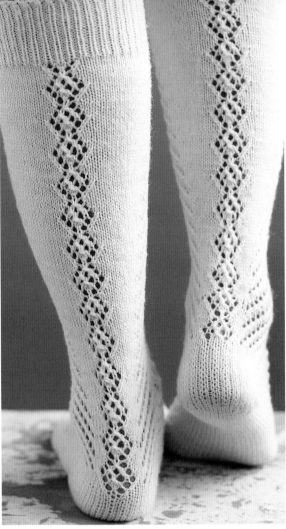

leg

Begin working in the round again. Work the stitches on needle 1 as set. Starting with the same row you worked on needle 1, work the Lace Chart over needle 2, placing a marker on each side of the center 9 stitches. Work 16 rounds in the pattern.

Next round: Between the markers on needle 2, increase 1 stitch by knitting a lifted increase into the bar between 2 stitches. Work the increases before the 1st stitch and after the last stitch inside the markers. You will increase 2 stitches in this manner every 6th round, working these extra stitches as knit stitches when you come to them on the next round.

NOTE: You will continue to work the first and last 8 (10, 12, 14) stitches and the center 9 stitches on needle 2 according to the Lace Chart as set as you knit the leg.

Continue to work the leg in the lace pattern as set, making the increases every 6 rounds as set, until you have 84 (88, 92, 96) stitches total on your needles.

Work without increasing until the sock measures 16" (40.5cm) or 2" (5cm) less than the desired finished length (measured from the bottom of the heel).

Work in k1, p1 ribbing for 2" (5cm).

Bind off loosely in rib. Weave in ends.

Finishing

If desired, wet block your Socks to the finished measurements. If you own sock blockers, slip dampened socks over the sock blockers until completely dry.

NOTE: I do not always block socks because they stretch out nicely while being worn; whether to block is up to you.

vintage kneesocks

Key

(blank)	K
O	YO
⼊	K2TOG
λ	SSK
⋏	SL1 K2TOG PSSO

Small Lace Chart

Row numbers (right side, odd): 1, 3, 5, 7, 9, 11, 13, 15, 17, 19, 21, 23, 25, 27, 29

Column numbers (bottom): 25, 23, 21, 19, 17, 15, 13, 11, 9, 7, 5, 3, 1

Medium Lace Chart

Row numbers (right side, odd): 1, 3, 5, 7, 9, 11, 13, 15, 17, 19, 21, 23, 25, 27, 29

Column numbers (bottom): 29, 27, 25, 23, 21, 19, 17, 15, 13, 11, 9, 7, 5, 3, 1

Large Lace Chart

Row numbers (right side, odd): 1, 3, 5, 7, 9, 11, 13, 15, 17, 19, 21, 23, 25, 27, 29

Column numbers (bottom): 33, 31, 29, 27, 25, 23, 21, 19, 17, 15, 13, 11, 9, 7, 5, 3, 1

Extra Large Lace Chart

Row numbers (right side, odd): 1, 3, 5, 7, 9, 11, 13, 15, 17, 19, 21, 23, 25, 27, 29

Column numbers (bottom): 37, 35, 33, 31, 29, 27, 25, 23, 21, 19, 17, 15, 13, 11, 9, 7, 5, 3, 1

RHOSSILI BEACH WATCH CAP

Several years ago while on a European vacation, I spent a day wandering down Rhossili Beach in the south of Wales. Despite the mid-July date, it was a raw, gray day with a chilly wind blowing. Hatless, I envied the fluffy lambs that dotted the nearby fields and wished for a snug woolly cap to keep my ears warm. My take on a simple classic ribbed watch cap was born from that day's experience. The cap features a deep ribbed cuff and an easy lace rib for the top. The pattern is written for a worsted-weight yarn and includes instructions for three head sizes, so you can warm up any head in a hurry.

Skill Level
Beginner

Size
Small (Medium, Large)

Finished Measurements
20$\frac{1}{4}$ (21$\frac{3}{4}$, 23$\frac{1}{2}$)" (51.5 [55, 59.5]cm) head circumference

Gauge
19 stitches and 24 rows = 4" (10cm) unblocked in stockinette stitch

Needles
US size 7 (4.5mm) 16" (40cm) circular needle and 1 set of 5 double-pointed needles, or size needed to attain gauge

Yarn
1 skein Dream in Color Classy, 100% superfine Australian superwash merino, 4 oz (113g), 250 yd (229m), Cloud Jungle
🄴 Worsted

Cap
cuff
Cast on 96 (104, 112) stitches on the circular needle. Join, being careful not to twist your stitches, and place a marker for the beginning of the round.

Work in rib pattern as follows: [K2, p1, k2, p3] 12 (13, 14) times.

Repeat this round until the cuff measures approximately 4$\frac{1}{2}$" (11.5cm) from the cast-on row.

start the lace pattern
Work the Lace Chart, repeating the 8 charted stitches 12 (13, 14) times around, or follow the written instructions:

Round 1: [Yo, ssk, k1, k2tog, yo, p3] 12 (13, 14) times.
Round 2: [K5, p3] 12 (13, 14) times.
Round 3: [K1, yo, s1 k2tog psso, yo, k1, p3] 12 (13, 14) times.
Round 4: Repeat round 2.

Work the Lace Chart as many times as necessary until your work measures approximately 9 (10, 11)" (23 [25.5, 28]cm) from the beginning.

shape the crown
Lace Decrease Round 1: [Work the first 5 stitches in the lace pattern as set, p1, p2tog] 12 (13, 14) times (12 [13, 14] stitches decreased; 84 [91, 98] stitches remain).
Next round: [K5, p2] 12 (13, 14) times.

Lace Decrease Round 2: [Work the first 5 stitches in the lace pattern as set, p2tog] 12 (13, 14) times (12 [13, 14] stitches decreased; 72 [78, 84] stitches remain).

Slip all stitches to 4 double-pointed needles, dividing the stitches evenly among the needles. At this point, you will stop working from the Lace Chart but continue to work decreases in stockinette stitch:

Round 1: [K4, k2tog] 12 (13, 14) times (60 [65, 70] stitches remain).

Round 2: [K3, k2tog] 12 (13, 14) times (48 [52, 56] stitches remain).

Round 3: [K2, k2tog] 12 (13, 14) times (36 [39, 42] stitches remain).

Round 4: [K1, k2tog] 12 (13, 14) times (24 [26, 28] stitches remain).

Round 5: [K2tog] 12 (13, 14) times (12 [13, 14] stitches remain).

Round 6: K2tog around (6 [7, 7] stitches remain).

NOTE: For the Medium size, end the round with k1. Break the working yarn, thread its end through a tapestry needle, weave the yarn through the live stitches twice, pull firmly to tighten, and fasten off on the wrong side. Weave in remaining ends.

Finishing

If desired, wet block your Cap to the finished measurements.

NOTE: Blocking is optional for this hat because, like socks, it will stretch out nicely while being worn.

rhossili beach watch cap

Key

	K
•	P
O	YO
⋏	K2TOG
⋋	SSK
⋏	SL1 K2TOG PSSO

Lace Chart

MAIRI TAM

A hat is a great way to try out knitting lace in the round because it is small enough to complete quickly and give you some instant gratification. Traditional Scottish tams are done in colorwork, but I think the style translates nicely to lacework as well. This tam uses fingering-weight wool, perfect for using up some sock yarn you might have lying around. It is a bit more challenging to make than the Rhossili Beach Watch Cap, so if you are new to knitting hats in the round, knit the cap first to hone your basic knitting skills.

Skill Level
Intermediate

Size
One size

Finished Measurements
11" (28cm) diameter

Gauge
6½ stitches and 8 rows = 1" (2.5cm) unblocked in stockinette stitch

Needles
US size 3 (3.25mm) 16" (40cm) circular needle and 1 set of 5 double-pointed needles, or size needed to attain gauge

Yarn
1 skein Dream in Color Smooshy Sock Yarn, 100% superfine Australian superwash merino, 4 oz (113g), 450 yd (412m), Beach Fog
1 Superfine

Ribbing
Using your favorite method, cast on 132 stitches onto the circular needle. Join, being careful not to twist your stitches, and begin to work in the round. Work in k2, p2 ribbing for 1½" (3.8cm).
Increase round: K9, [k1, m1, k2, m1] 19 times, k9, [k1, m1, k2, m1] 19 times (208 stitches total).

Tam
Set up round: [K26, place marker] 8 times (8 sections marked).
Rounds 1–36: Work Chart A across each 26-stitch section 8 times.
Rounds 37–63: Work Chart B across each of the 8 sections. (Slip stitches from your circular needle to double-pointed needles when the circumference of your work becomes too small to fit on the circular needle.)

After completing all 27 rounds of Chart B, you will have 8 stitches on your needles.
Next round: K2tog 4 times (4 stitches remain).

I-Cord
Slip the remaining 4 stitches onto a double-pointed needle and knit across. Do not turn your work; slide the stitches to the other end of the needle and knit the row again without turning, pulling the working yarn tight behind the stitches. Continue in this manner until the cord measures 1" (2.5cm) or the desired length.
Break the working yarn, thread its tail through a tapestry needle, weave the yarn through the live stitches twice, pull firmly to tighten, and fasten off on the wrong side. Weave in ends.

Finishing

Soak the Tam in tepid water for at least 20 minutes, then roll in a towel and gently squeeze out excess water. Slip your dampened Tam over an 11" (28cm) dinner plate, shaping it carefully so that the head opening is centered on the underside of the plate. (Alternatively, lay your Tam on a flat surface and spread it into shape.) Allow the Tam to dry completely.

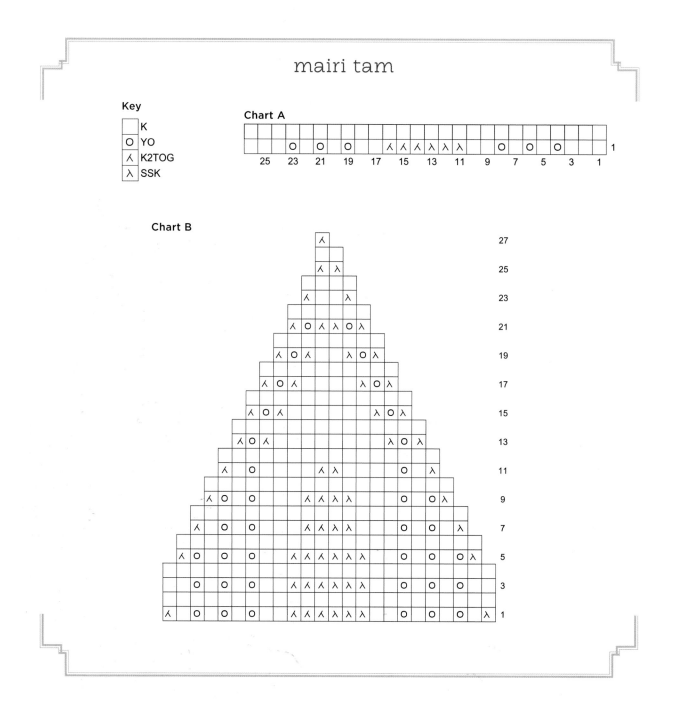

mairi tam

Key

	K
O	YO
⋏	K2TOG
⋋	SSK

Chart A

Chart B

LIGHT-AS-A-FEATHER SMOKE RING

This luxurious, lacy cowl is another design that beginners will love.
It's a great introduction to using lace-weight yarn because the needles are
large and the lace pattern simple. The pattern calls for 1 skein of a silk–cashmere
blend but requires only about half of one 400-yd (366-m) skein. Consider splurging
on a single skein of a more exotic fiber like cashmere, silk, alpaca, or qiviut
to really treat someone (or yourself!).

Skill Level
Beginner

Size
One size

Finished Measurements
23$\frac{1}{2}$" (59.5cm) circumference,
8" (20.5cm) high (from edge to
edge)

Gauge
5 stitches and 6 rows = 1" (2.5cm)
unblocked in stockinette stitch

Needles
US size 5 (3.75mm) 16" (40cm)
circular needle, or size needed to
attain gauge

Yarn
1 skein Jade Sapphire Silk
Cashmere, 55% silk and 45%
cashmere, 1.9 oz (55g), 400 yd
(366m), Amethyst Haze
(1) Superfine

NOTE: Adjust the circumference of the cowl by adding or deleting
stitches in increments of 9 (the 9-stitch pattern repeat) and the height
by knitting more or fewer rounds. If you change the size, keep in mind
that your yarn requirements may change.

Cowl
Using the Lace Cast-On, loosely cast on 117
stitches. Join, being careful not to twist your
stitches, and knit 1 round.

start the lace pattern
Work row 1 of the 9-stitch Lace Chart 13 times
around.
Then, work rows 2, 3, and 4. On odd-numbered
rounds work the lace pattern and on even-
numbered rounds, knit around.

Continue working the lace pattern, working all 4
rows of the Lace Chart until your piece measures
8" (20.5cm) or your desired length, ending after
working row 2 or 4.
Bind off loosely using the Russian Bind-Off. Weave
in ends.

Finishing
Steam block or wet block your Cowl to the finished
measurements.

light-as-a-feather
smoke ring

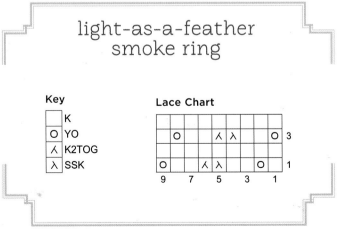

Key

	K
O	YO
⅄	K2TOG
λ	SSK

Lace Chart

GARDEN PARTY CARDIGAN

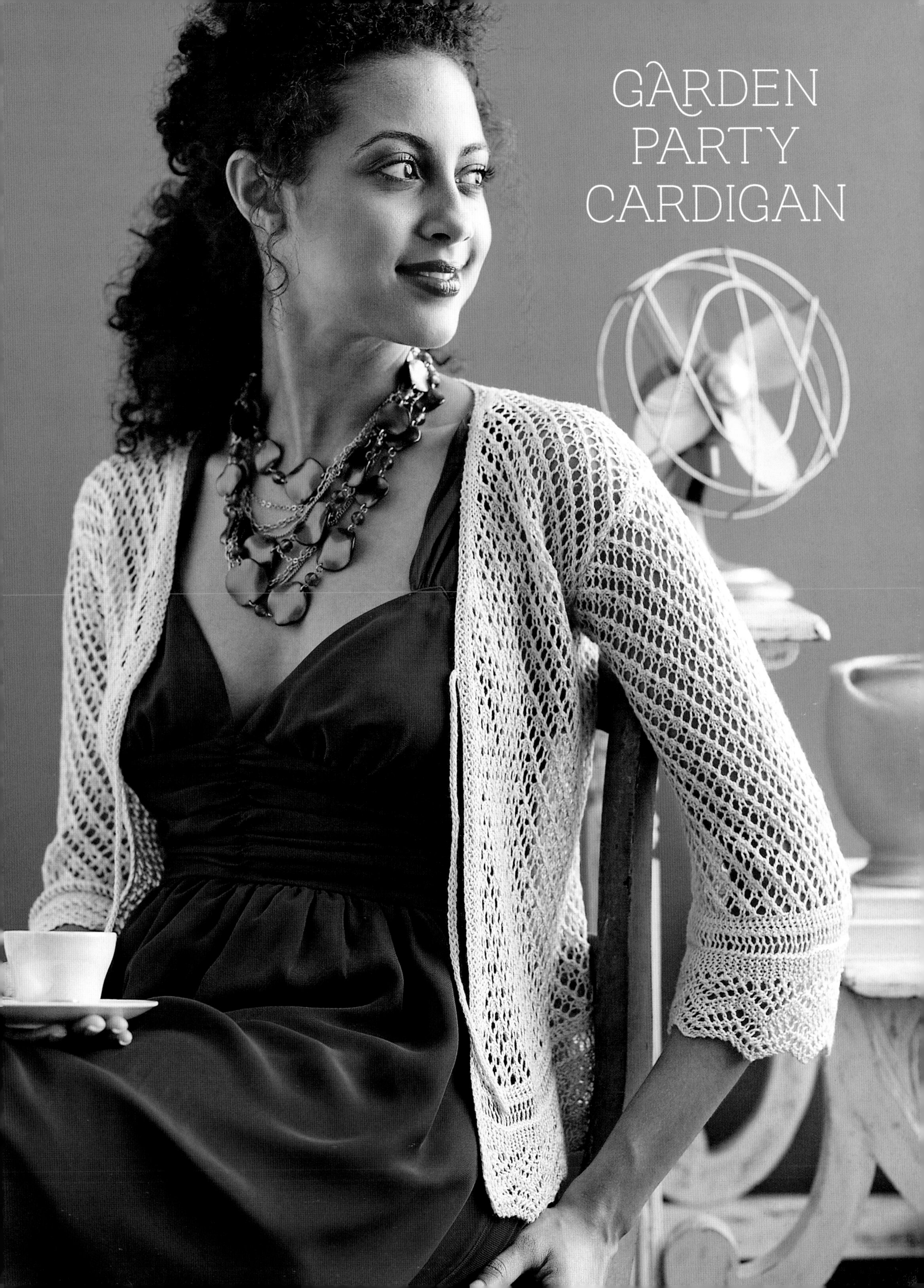

GARDEN PARTY CARDIGAN

This sweet silk cardigan is perfect to slip on over a summer party dress—but don't knit this pattern only for an elegant soiree. Substitute a fine cotton-blend yarn to make a cardigan equally appropriate for the office or a silk–mohair blend to make a warmer version for winter. Although I have designated the skill level of this pattern as advanced because of the edging technique used, the stitches are easy and the shaping is simple—you can make this pretty cardigan your own for any season.

Skill Level
Advanced

Size
Women's Small (Medium, Large, Extra Large)

Finished Measurements
37 (42$\frac{1}{2}$, 48, 53)" (94, [108, 122, 134.5]cm) bust circumference, 20 (20, 21$\frac{1}{2}$, 21$\frac{1}{2}$)" (51, [51, 54.5, 54.5]cm) long

Gauge
4$\frac{1}{2}$ stitches and 8 rows = 1" (2.5cm) blocked over lace pattern

Needles
US size 3 (3.25mm) 24" (60cm) circular needle and 2 double-pointed needles, or size needed to attain gauge

Yarn
3 (4, 4, 5) skeins Tilli Tomas Vol de la Mer, 70% silk, 30% Seacell, 1$\frac{3}{4}$ oz (50g), 290 yd (265m), Natural (**1**) Superfine

Edging
Cast on 18 stitches.
Work all 16 rows of the Edging Chart 21 (24, 27, 30) times.
Bind off all stitches, but do not break the working yarn.

Body
With the working yarn, pick up 168 (192, 216, 240) stitches along the long, straight side of the Edging. (Pick up 1 stitch in each of the slipped edge stitches—that is, 8 stitches total along the top of each repeat of the Edging.)
Next row (WS): Purl across.

start the lace pattern
Work the Body Chart, working the 4-stitch pattern repeat 40 (46, 52, 58) times.

Work all 8 rows of the Body Chart as many times as needed until the piece measures 12 (12, 13, 13)" (30.5, [30.5, 33, 33]cm) from the bottom of the edging (or your desired length to the armholes), ending after completing a wrong-side (even-numbered) row.

divide for the armholes and increase
Continuing in the Body Chart, work 41 (47, 53, 59) stitches, increase 1, k1. Put the remainder of the stitches on a length of waste yarn.

work the right front
Work 43 (49, 55, 61) stitches for right front as follows:
Next row (WS): Purl across.
Decrease row (RS): K1, ssk (neck edge), work in lace pattern as set to end of row.

Next row (WS): Purl across.

Repeat the decrease row every other row 3 (5, 7, 9) times more, then every 4th row 9 times (30 [34, 38, 42] stitches remain after the last repeat).

Work even in lace pattern as set until armhole measures 8 (8, 8½, 8½)" (20.5, [20.5, 21.5, 21.5]cm), ending with a wrong-side row.

Bind off all stitches with the right side facing. Weave in ends.

work the back

With the right side facing, slip the next 84 (96, 108, 120) stitches from the waste yarn back onto the needle.

Next row (RS): Increase 1, work in pattern as set to last stitch, increase 1 (86 [98, 110, 122] stitches). Keeping the 1st and last stitch of each row in stockinette stitch, work even in lace pattern as set until the back matches the right front armhole length, ending with a wrong-side row.

Bind off all stitches with the right side facing. Weave in ends.

work the left front

Slip the remaining 42 (48, 54, 60) stitches from the waste yarn back onto the needle.

Next row (RS): Increase 1, work in pattern as set to end of row (43 [49, 55, 61] stitches).

Next row (WS): Purl across.

Decrease row (RS): Work to last 3 stitches, k2tog, k1.

Next row (WS): Purl across.

Repeat the decrease row every other row 3 (5, 7, 9) times more, then every 4th row 9 times (30 [34, 38, 42] stitches remain after the last repeat).

Work even in lace pattern as set until armhole measures 8 (8, 8½, 8½)" (20.5, [20.5, 21.5, 21.5]cm), ending with a wrong-side row.

Bind off all stitches with the right side facing. Weave in ends.

Sleeve (Make 2)

Cast on 18 stitches.

Work the Edging Chart 9 (9, 10, 10) times in the same manner as for the Edging on the bottom of the Body.

Bind off all stitches, but do not break the working yarn.

With the working yarn, pick up 72 (72, 80, 80) stitches along the long, straight side of the Edging. (Pick up 1 stitch in each of the slipped edge stitches—that is, 8 stitches total along the top of each repeat of the Edging.)

Work in the lace pattern from the Body Chart until the piece measures 12" (30.5cm) from the bottom of the edging (or your desired length for the Sleeve).

Bind off. Weave in ends.

Finishing

Steam block or wet block the Body and the Sleeves to the finished measurements.
Sew the Body together at the shoulders.

work the front and neck edging

With the right side facing, pick up and knit approximately 54 (54, 58, 58) stitches from the bottom of the left front to the beginning of the V-neck, 50 (50, 54, 54) stitches up the left side neck, 30 stitches around the back of the neck, 50 (50, 54, 54) stitches down the right side neck, and 54 (54, 58, 58) stitches down the right front.

Working back and forth, knit 2 rows.
Bind off knitwise.

Fold each Sleeve in half lengthwise and sew the edges together. Set each Sleeve into its armhole, easing it to fit, and sew it in place.

i-cord ties

On 1 side of the V-neck, where the neckline begins, pick up and knit 3 stitches using a circular needle or double-pointed needles. Do not turn your work; slide the stitches to the other end of the needle and knit the row again without turning, pulling the working yarn tight behind the stitches.

Continue in this manner until the I-cord measures 12" (30.5cm).

Bind off all stitches.
Repeat on the other side to match.
Weave in all remaining ends.

NOTE: Instead of knitting I-cord ties, crochet ties or attach ribbon ties.

garden party cardigan

Body

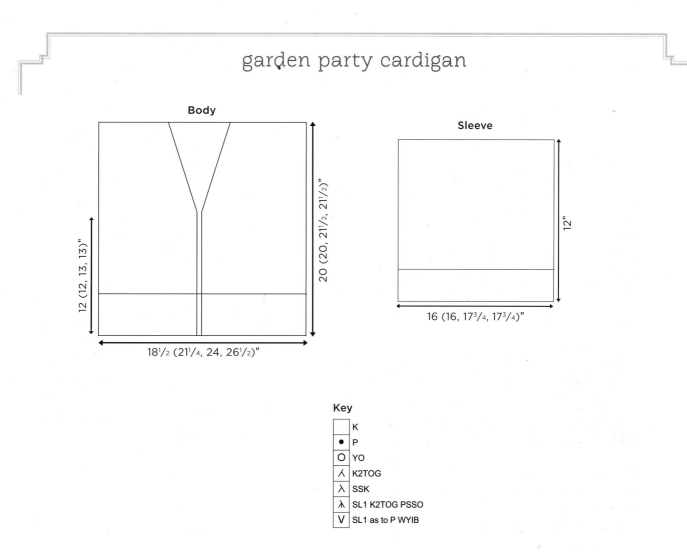

20 (20, 21½, 21½)"

12 (12, 13, 13)"

18½ (21¼, 24, 26½)"

Sleeve

12"

16 (16, 17¾, 17¾)"

Key

	K
•	P
O	YO
⋏	K2TOG
λ	SSK
λ	SL1 K2TOG PSSO
V	SL1 as to P WYIB

Edging Chart

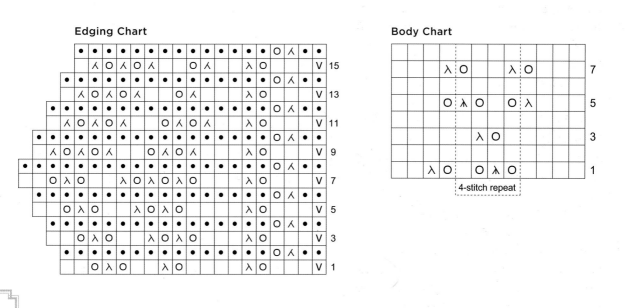

Body Chart

4-stitch repeat

SEASHELL CAMI

With its bottom border pattern reminiscent of seashells, this camisole would be just the thing for the fashionable mermaid or water nymph. It makes me think of a sandy beach, with the small lace pattern representing the foam of the receding surf. This body-hugging piece is knit from a lightweight yarn that blends merino wool with Seacell, but you can substitute any fingering-weight cotton or silk blend yarn that knits to gauge.

Skill Level
Advanced

Size
Extra Small (Small, Medium, Large)

Finished Measurements
34$\frac{1}{2}$ (37$\frac{3}{4}$, 41, 44$\frac{1}{2}$)" (88 [96, 104, 113]cm) bust circumference, 22 (22$\frac{1}{2}$, 24, 24$\frac{1}{2}$)" (56 [57, 61, 62]cm) long

Gauge
7 stitches and 9 rows = 1" (2.5cm) unblocked in lace pattern

Needles
1 US size 2 (3mm) 24" to 32" (60 to 80cm) circular needle, or size needed to attain gauge, and one 24" to 32" (60 to 80cm) circular needle 1 size larger

Yarn
2 (2, 2, 3) skeins Hand Maiden Swiss Mountain Sea Sock, 51% Silk, 29% superwash merino, 20% Seacell, 3$\frac{1}{2}$ oz (100g), 436 yd (399m), Topaz **1** Superfine

Bottom Border
Using the larger needle, cast on 240 (264, 288, 312) stitches.
Join, being careful not to twist stitches, and begin to work in the round.
Work the Border Chart 20 (22, 24, 26) times around.
Continue to work all 25 rows of the Border Chart.

Body
Change to the smaller needle and work the Body Chart 40 (44, 48, 52) times around.
Work all 4 rows of the Body Chart until the piece measures 13 (13$\frac{1}{2}$, 14, 14$\frac{1}{2}$)" (33 [34.5, 35.5, 37]cm) from the cast-on edge, ending after working an even-numbered row.

shape the top
Leave the first 60 (66, 72, 78) stitches on the needle and slip the remaining 180 (198, 216, 234) stitches to a stitch holder or a length of waste yarn.
NOTE: From this point forward, you will knit back and forth on the stitches on the needle; odd-numbered rows are the right side, and even-numbered rows are the wrong side.
Row 1 (RS): K2, k2tog, work in lace pattern to last 4 stitches, ssk, k2 (2 stitches decreased).
Row 2 (WS): K2, purl to last 2 stitches, k2.
Repeat these 2 rows, working in the pattern as set, until 28 (32, 36, 40) stitches remain.
Row 1 (RS): K2, k2tog, work in pattern to last 4 stitches, ssk, k2 (2 stitches decreased).
Row 2 (WS): K2, p2tog, purl to last 4 stitches, p2tog tbl, k2 (2 stitches decreased).

Repeat these 2 rows, working in the pattern as set, until 6 stitches remain.

Slip the remaining 6 stitches onto a stitch holder or a length of waste yarn. (The knitted piece should be shaped like a triangle.)

Slip the next 60 (66, 72, 78) stitches from the stitch holder to the needle and work from Shape the Top to create another triangle.

Repeat this instruction twice more.

Straps

Place the 6 stitches from 1 of the front triangles onto the smaller circular needle and, with the right side facing, knit across. Work back and forth, knitting each row until the strap is 12 (12, 13, 13)" (30.5 [30.5, 33, 33]cm) long or long enough to fit comfortably over the shoulder and attach to the top of the corresponding triangle on the back.

NOTE: Because of the fine gauge and yarn, the fabric stretches significantly, and I recommend that you try it on as you knit the straps to ensure a good fit and that you stretch it as you measure. If you knit this pattern as a gift, use a ready-made tank top or camisole as a guide for the strap lengths.

Work a 2nd strap on the 2nd front triangle to match, then graft the 6 stitches at the end of each strap to the 6 live stitches on each of the back triangles. Weave in ends.

Finishing

Reinforce the 4 V-shapes on the body of the Cami where you start the decrease for the triangles: Turn the piece inside out. Using a length of the project yarn, carefully sew together the stitches on each side of the bottom of each V. Weave in ends. Steam block or wet block the Cami to the finished measurements.

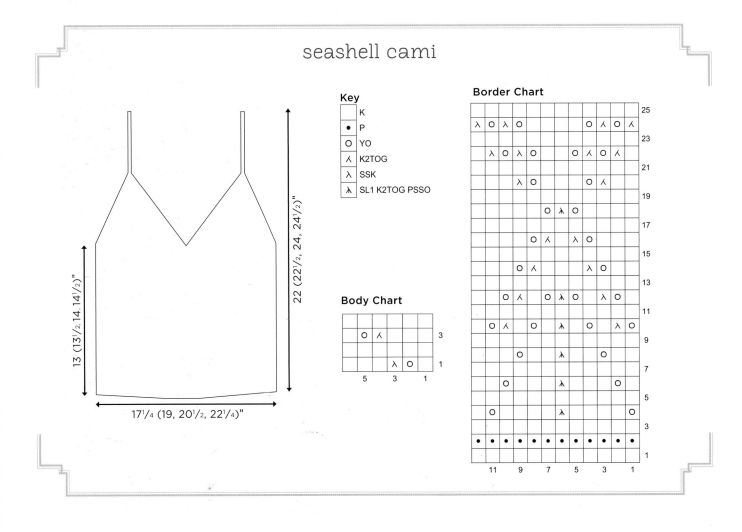

seashell cami

DEIRDRE SWEATER

Someone as fascinated by lace as I am can't help but see the world through "lace eyes." That's what happened with this pullover sweater, originally designed to showcase vertical cable motifs. Luckily, it looks just as good in lace—and will still keep you warm in chilly weather. The basic design and lace motif are simple, appropriate for a knitter who is new to lace but ready to incorporate shaping into her work.

Skill Level
Adventuresome Intermediate

Size
Women's Extra Small (Small, Medium, Large, Extra Large)

Finished Measurements
35 (38, 41, 44, 47)" (89 [96.5, 104, 112, 119.5]cm) bust circumference, 24 (24½, 24½, 25, 25½)" (61 [62, 62, 63.5, 65]cm) long

Gauge
27 stitches and 32 rows per 4" (10cm) in lace pattern on smaller needles (Be sure to check your gauge for this design. Calmer is a stretchy yarn and may require some swatching to find the proper needle size for the stated gauge.)

Needles
US size 6 (4mm) or one 24" (60cm) circular needle, or size needed to attain gauge, and 2 double-pointed needles 1 size larger

Yarn
9 (10, 11, 12, 13) skeins Rowan Calmer, 75% cotton, 25% microfiber, 1¾ oz (50g), 175 yd (160m), Garnet **3** Light

NOTE: When you work the "increase 1" for the Back, you can do a lifted increase between 2 stitches.

Back
Using a long-tail cast-on, cast on 117 (128, 139, 150, 161) stitches. Set up pattern as follows:

Row 1 (RS): P1, work row 1 of the Lace Chart 10 (11, 12, 13, 14) times, p6.

Row 2 (WS): K6, work row 2 of the Lace Chart 10 (11, 12, 13, 14) times, k1.

Rows 3–13: Continue in this manner, keeping the border stitches and working all 4 rows of the Lace Chart until you have worked 13 rows total (ending after having worked row 1 of the Lace Chart).

Row 14 (WS): K1, k2tog tbl, work in lace pattern to last 3 stitches, k2tog, k1 (115 [126, 137, 148, 159] stitches total).

Rows 15–27: Work 13 rows in pattern as set, incorporating the decreases you worked on row 14 into the pattern.

Row 28: K5, p6, k1, k2tog tbl, work in lace pattern to last 14 stitches, k2tog, k1, p6, k5 (113 [124, 135, 146, 157] stitches total).

Rows 29–41: Work 13 rows, incorporating the decreases you worked on row 28 into the pattern.

Row 42: K5, p6, k4, p6, k1, k2tog tbl, work in lace pattern to the last 24 stitches, k2tog, k1, p6, k4, p6, k5 (111 [122, 133, 144, 155] stitches total).

Rows 43–57: Work 15 rows, incorporating the decreases you worked on row 42 into the pattern.

Row 58: K5, p6, [k4, p6] twice, k1, k2tog tbl, work in

pattern to last 34 stitches, k2tog, k1, (p6, k4) twice, p6, k5 (109 [120, 131, 142, 153] stitches total).

Rows 59–71: Work 13 rows in pattern as set, taking the decreases you worked on row 58 into the pattern.

Row 72: K5, p6, [k4, p6] twice, k2, increase 1, work in pattern to last 34 stitches, k2, increase 1, k1, [p6, k4] twice, p6, k5 (111 [122, 133, 144, 155] stitches total).

Rows 73–85: Work 13 rows, incorporating the increases you worked on row 72 into the pattern.

Row 86: K5, p6, k4, p6, k2, increase 1, work in pattern to last 24 stitches, k2, increase 1, k1, p6, k4, p6, k5 (113 [124, 135, 146, 157] stitches total).

Rows 87–99: Work 13 rows in pattern as set, incorporating the increases you worked on row 86 into the pattern.

Row 100: K5, p6, k2, increase 1, work in pattern to last 14 stitches, k2, increase 1, k1, p6, k5 (115 [126, 137, 148, 159] stitches total).

Rows 101–115: Work 15 rows in pattern as set, incorporating the increases you worked on row 100 into the pattern.

Row 116: K2, increase 1, work in pattern to the last 3 stitches, increase 1, k2 (117 [128, 139, 150, 161] stitches total).

Continue to work the pattern as set until the piece measures 14¹⁄₂ (15, 15, 15¹⁄₂, 16)" (37 [38, 38, 39.5, 40.5] cm) from the cast-on edge.

shape armholes
Bind off 9 (10, 10, 11, 12) stitches at the beginning of the next 2 rows.

Decrease 1 stitch at each end of the row, working the beginning-of-the-row decreases as k2tog and the end-of-the-row decreases as k2tog tbl, every other row, 9 times.

Continue in the pattern as set until the piece measures 23½ (24, 24, 24½, 25)" (59.5 [61, 61, 62, 63.5]cm) from the cast-on edge.

shape shoulders

Bind off 7 (8, 8, 9, 9) stitches at the beginning of the next 2 rows.

Bind off 8 (9, 9, 10, 10) stitches at the beginning of the next 4 rows.

Bind off the remaining 35 (38, 49, 52, 61) back neck stitches.

Front

Work as for the Back, including all shaping, and, *at the same time*, when the piece measures 21 (21½, 21½, 22, 22½)" (53.5 [54.5, 54.5, 56, 57]cm), begin the neck shaping as follows:

Work to the center 11 (12, 15, 16, 17) stitches, drop the working yarn, attach another ball of yarn. Bind off the center 11 (12, 15, 16, 17) stitches, work to the end of the row.

Working both sides of the neck at the same time, from different balls of yarn:

Bind off 2 stitches at each neck edge 3 (4, 5, 6, 7) times.

Decrease 1 stitch at each neck edge, every other row, 6 (5, 7, 6, 8) times.

Continue to work in the pattern as set until the piece measures 23½ (24, 24, 24½, 25)" (59.5 [61, 61, 62.5, 63.5]cm) from the cast-on edge.

Work the shoulder shaping at shoulder edges to correspond with the back shoulder shaping.

Sleeve (Make 2)

Using a long-tail cast-on, cast on 64 stitches. Set up the pattern as follows:

Row 1 (RS): K2, work row 1 of the Lace Chart 5 times, p5, k2.

Row 2: P2, k5, work row 2 of the Lace Chart 5 times, p2.

Increase 1 stitch by working a lifted increase inside the edge stitch on each side every 4th row 20 (21, 21, 22, 23) times, and then every 6th row 8 times; work extra repeats of the Lace Chart as the Sleeve width grows (120 [122, 122, 124, 126] stitches total after the last increase row).

Continue in the pattern as set until the piece measures 17 (17½, 17½, 18, 18)" (43 [44.5, 44.5, 45.5, 45.5]cm) from the cast-on edge.

shape the sleeve cap

Bind off 9 (10, 10, 11, 12) stitches at the beginning of the next 2 rows.

Decrease 1 stitch on each side, every other row, 11 (11, 11, 14, 14) times.

Decrease 1 stitch on each side, every row, 20 (20, 20, 17, 17) times.

NOTE: Work the beginning-of-the-row decreases as k2tog and the end-of-the-row decreases as k2tog tbl.

Bind off 5 stitches at the beginning of the next 4 rows.

Bind off the remaining 20 stitches. Weave in ends.

Finishing

Block all pieces to the finished measurements.

i-cord neck edging

Sew the Front and Back together at the shoulders. Using a circular needle in the same size as used for the Body of the sweater and with the right side facing, knit the 35 (38, 49, 52, 61) back neck stitches and *k2tog in the center of each lace motif* as you work the stitches, pick up and knit 24 stitches down the left side front, knit across the center 11 (12, 15, 16, 17) stitches and *k2tog in the center of each lace motif* as you work the stitches, pick up and knit 24 stitches up the right side front.

Work an applied I-cord edging: After the last picked-up stitch, use the working yarn and a backward loop cast-on to cast on 3 stitches to a double-pointed needle one size larger than the needle size used to knit the Body. Turn the work. Knit across.

Knit the first 2 stitches from this double-pointed needle onto a 2nd double-pointed needle.

Slip the 3rd unworked stitch from the 1st needle onto the 2nd needle, and slip the 1st unworked neck stitch from the circular needle next to the unworked stitch on the 2nd double-pointed needle. Insert the tip of the 1st (now empty) double-pointed needle through the back loops of the 2 unworked stitches, and knit them together.

Slide the 3 stitches to the other end of the double-pointed needle and continue to work I-cord rounds, knitting the last of the 3 stitches together with 1 stitch from the neck.

After all edge stitches from the neck have been attached to the I-cord edging, sew the ends of the I-cord together. Weave in ends.

Fit the sleeve caps into the armholes and sew them into place. Sew up the side and sleeve seams.

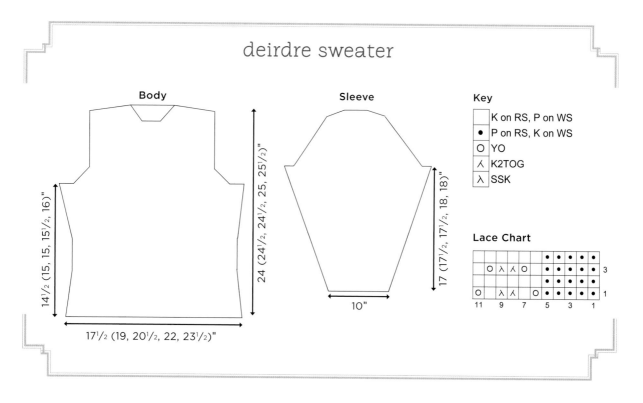

deirdre sweater

Body

Sleeve

Key

	K on RS, P on WS
●	P on RS, K on WS
O	YO
⋏	K2TOG
λ	SSK

14½ (15, 15, 15½, 16)"

17½ (19, 20½, 22, 23½)"

24 (24½, 24½, 25, 25½)"

10"

17 (17½, 17½, 18, 18)"

Lace Chart

RESOURCES

This section contains various useful tidbits of information, including sources for the yarns used to knit the sample projects, a chart of standard yarn weights, a list of the abbreviations used and their definitions, and a master key to the symbols used in the charts.

YARNS

All of the projects in this book call for materials that are readily available at local yarn stores and online. However, if you have trouble finding a product needed to complete a project in the book, consult the supplier's website, listed here, to locate a convenient distributor.

Alchemy Yarns of Transformation
www.alchemyyarns.com
707-823-3276

Cascade Yarns
www.cascadeyarns.com

Cherry Tree Hill
www.cherryyarn.com
802-525-3311

Dream in Color
www.dreamincoloryarn.com
dream@dreamincoloryarn.com

Fiesta Yarns
www.fiestayarns.com
505-892-5008

Green Mountain Spinnery
www.spinnery.com
802-387-4528

Handmaiden Fine Yarn
www.handmaiden.ca
handmaiden@fleeceartist.com

Jade Sapphire
www.jadesapphire.com
845-215-9946

Jojoland International, LLC
www.jojoland.com
972-624-8990

Madelinetosh
www.madelinetosh.com
817-249-3066

Rowan
www.knitrowan.com
+44 (0) 1484 681881

Shibui Knits, LLC
www.shibuiknits.com
503-595-5898

Tilli Tomas
www.tillitomas.com
617-524-3330

STANDARD YARN WEIGHT SYSTEM

Categories of yarn, gauge ranges, and recommended needle and hook sizes.

CYCA	1	2	3	4	5
Yarn Weight	Lace, Fingering, Sock	Sport	DK, Light Worsted	Worsted, Aran	Chunky
Avg. Knitted Gauge over 4" (10cm)	27–32 sts	23–26 sts	21–24 sts	16–20 sts	12–15 sts
Recommended Needle in US Size Range	1–3	3–5	5–7	7–9	9–11
Recommended Needle in Metric Size Range	2.25–3.25mm	3.25–3.75mm	3.75–4.5mm	4.5–5.5mm	5.5–8mm

ABBREVIATIONS

INC—increase

K—knit

K2TOG—knit 2 together (decrease 1 stitch)

K3 in 1 ST—knit 3 in 1 stitch (increase 2 stitches) (K1 into the front loop of the next stitch, k1 into the back loop of the same stitch, k1 into the front loop of the stitch again, and slide the 3 knitted stitches to the right-hand needle.)

KFB—knit into the front and back of the stitch (increase 1 stitch)

M1—make 1 (increase 1 stitch)

P—purl

P2TOG—purl 2 together (decrease 1 stitch)

PFB—purl into the front and back of the stitch (increase 1 stitch)

PSSO—pass slipped stitch over (decrease 1 stitch)

RS—right side

SL(1)—slip (Pass the stitch from the left-hand needle to the right-hand needle without working it. May be worked knitwise [with needle inserted left to right] or purlwise [with needle inserted right to left].)

SSK—slip, slip, knit (decrease 1 stitch) (Slip 1 stitch as if to knit, then slip the next stitch as if to purl. Insert the left-hand needle into the front loops of the slipped stitches and knit them together from this position, that is, through the back loops.)

ST(s)—stitch(es)

WS—wrong side

WYIB—with yarn in back of work

WYIF—with yarn in front of work

W&T—wrap and turn (Bring yarn to front of work between needles, slip the next stitch to the right-hand needle, bring yarn around this stitch to the back of the work, slip the stitch back to the left-hand needle, and turn your work to begin working back in the other direction.)

YO—yarn over (increase 1 stitch) (See Part 2 [page 21] for the many varieties of yarn overs you can make.)

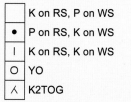 KEY TO SYMBOLS

All of the symbols used in all of the charts in this book are defined in the following key.

☐	K on RS, P on WS	λ	SSK	⋁	SL1 as to P WYIF
•	P on RS, K on WS	λ	SL1 K2TOG PSSO	V	SL1 as to P WYIB
I	K on RS, K on WS	⊿	P2TOG	ŏ	INC 1
O	YO	⏀	Make bobble (see instructions, Bobble Gloves)	⊓	K3 in 1 ST (INC 2 STS)
⋏	K2TOG	U	K1TOG with 1 ST from body		

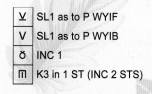

ACKNOWLEDGMENTS

Thank you to my publisher Potter Craft for creating consistently beautiful, high-quality books from my scribbles and doodles. I owe special thanks to Betty Wong for all her hard work and help during the process of creating this book.

Thank you to my editor, Rebecca Behan, who always has wonderful ideas for improving my writing and who makes the editing and rewrite process almost a pleasure.

Thanks also to the wonderful knitters who tested my patterns and knit the samples for photography: Aimee M. Abernathy, Timmie Ballard, Frances Clement, Alice Coppa, Muriel Correa, Janice Fischer, Sharon Hart, Lindsey-Brooke Hessa, Johanne Ländin, Laura Linneman, Stacy Little, Keri Lloyd, Karen L. Rubin, Isobel Thomas, and Leslie Thompson. All of these women are talented knitters, and I am proud to call them my friends.

A special thanks to Sharon Hart who took on extra knitting at the last minute and did a fantastic job of working through a Pattern from Hell with me.

Thank you to Ian Ories who took the many, many photographs used to create the illustrations of techniques demonstrated in this book—and got them all in one take.

Thank you to Sheri Berger at The Loopy Ewe, who supplied much of the yarn used to knit the samples for this book and who responded quickly and cheerfully to the inevitable yarn emergency.

Thank you to Alana Henry for creating the schematics for the three sweater designs.

And last but not least, my heartfelt thanks to my technical editor and very good friend Lindsey-Brooke Hessa. Turning my patterns over to L-B gives me a warm fuzzy feeling because she does such a thorough job of proofing, critiquing, and checking my patterns. As an example of her devotion to her work, L-B knit the True Love Scarf not once but twice to check the clarity and accuracy of the pattern.

PROJECT INDEX

Lace Stripe Scarf (page 40)

Elizabeth's Cowl (page 43)

Cranbourne Scarf (page 46)

True Love Scarf (page 50)

True Love Stole (page 50)

Stacy Shawl   (page 58)

Two-Thirds Shawl (page 64)

Tiffany Triangle Shawl (page 68)

Vortex Spiral Shawl   (page 74)

Vortex Spiral Afghan (page 74)

Poor Poet's Mitts (page 82)

Esplanade Mittens (page 86)

PROJECT INDEX

Bobble Gloves (page 92)

Delicate Vines Socks (page 97)

Diamond Lace Socks (page 102)

Vintage Kneesocks (page 107)

Rhossili Beach Watch Cap (page 112)

Mairi Tam (page 116)

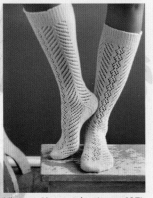

Light-as-a-Feather Smoke Ring
(page 120)

Garden Party Cardigan (page 123)

Seashell Cami   (page 128)

Deirdre Sweater (page 132)

INDEX

Note: Page numbers in *italics* indicate patterns.